Treasu

Here is a treasure chest c
with poems, stories, ridd
games to play and thing
and fairies, funny animal
adventures. Some things are serious and some are amusing, to suit your mood, but all are fun. So if it's a wet day, or you want something different to do, whether you are by yourself or with your friends, delve into this treasure store and see what special gems it holds for you.

Jennifer Curry has written lots of books for children, including *Pleasure Trove*, in Beavers, and *This is the Way We Sow and Grow*, *How Did It Start* and *Collecting* – all published by Hamlyn.

TREASURE TROVE

Jennifer Curry

Illustrated by John Speirs

Beaver Books

First published in 1977 by
The Hamlyn Publishing Group Limited
London · New York · Sydney · Toronto
Astronaut House, Feltham, Middlesex, England

ISBN 0 600 38752 6

Printed in England by Cox & Wyman Limited
London, Reading and Fakenham
Set in Monotype Bembo

ACKNOWLEDGEMENTS

The author and publishers would like to thank the following people for giving permission to include in this anthology material which is their copyright. The publishers have made very effort to trace copyright holders. If we have inadvertently omitted to acknowledge anyone we should be most grateful if this could be brought to our attention for correction at the first opportunity.

Kenneth Agar for 'Advice to a Cannibal' from *Nothing Solemn*, published by Evans Brothers
Angus and Robertson Publishers, Sydney, for 'Woolloomooloo' by C. J. Dennis, from *A Book for Kids*
Associated Book Publishers Limited for 'My Uncle Paul of Pimlico' from *Rhymes Without Reason* by Mervyn Peake
Associated Book Publishers Limited and Curtis Brown Limited for 'Family Holiday', from *Drawn from Memory* by Ernest Shepard
Barrie & Jenkins for 'A Country Bedroom' by Frances Cornford, from *Collected Poems*
Leonard Clark for 'Our Family', from *Collected Poems and Verses for Children*, published by Dennis Dobson
J. M. Dent & Sons Limited and the Trustees for the Copyrights of the late Dylan Thomas for the extract from *Quite Early One Morning*
Dennis Dobson Publishers for 'The ABC' from *The Little Pot Boiler* by Spike Milligan
Duckworth and Company Limited for 'The Python' by Hilaire Belloc, from *More Beasts for Worse Children*
George Elvey for the extract from *A Norwegian Childhood*, taken from *A Golden Land*, published by Longman
Evans Brothers Limited for 'A Lot of . . .' and 'North Wind's Winter Recipe for the Cold', from *Word Spinning*
Faber and Faber Limited for 'Wit Wit Willy Willy, from *Without Knowing Mr Walkley* by Edith Olivier
Robert Graves and Cassell and Company for 'The Six Badgers' from *Collected Poems*
Hamish Hamilton Children's Books Limited for 'The Beaver' from *Zoo Doings and other poems* by Jack Prelutsky

William Heinemann Limited for 'Jargon' by James Reeves
David Higham Associates Limited for 'Cottage' by Eleanor Farjeon, from *Puffin Quartet of Poets*, published by Penguin Books Limited; and for 'Wart Meets Merlyn' from *The Sword in the Stone* by T. H. White, published by Collins
David Higham Associates Limited and Chatto & Windus for 'Snowflakes' by Clive Sansom, from *An English Year*
Hogarth Press Limited for 'Summer Day' from *Cider With Rosie* by Laurie Lee
Hogarth Press Limited and the Literary Estate of Virginia Woolf for 'Children Waking' from *The Waves* by Virginia Woolf
James Hurley for 'Greedy Dog'
Kaye & Ward Limited for the extract from *Fun With Picture Projects* by Tony Hart. Copyright © Kaye & Ward Ltd 1973
James Kirkup for 'The Dripping Tap'
George Macbeth for 'The Red Herring' from *A Doomsday Book*, published by Macmillan Limited
James MacGibbon for 'My Cats' by Stevie Smith
Macmillan Limited for 'Two's Company' from *Rhyme and Rhythm* by Raymond Wilson
Macmillan Limited and Macmillan Company of Canada for 'Weathers' from *Collected Poems* by Thomas Hardy
Macmillan Limited and Curtis Brown Limited for 'How Many Miles' by Clyde Watson, from *Father Fox's Pennyrhymes*
John Travers Moore for 'Springburst' from *There's Motion Everywhere*, published by Houghton Mifflin Company
Pitman Publishing Limited for 'Animals' by Kathleen Bartlett, from *Number Rhymes and Finger Plays* by E. R. Boyce and K. Bartlett
Alastair Reid for 'A Spell for Sleeping' from *A Golden Land*, published by Longman
Alexander Resnikoff for 'Two Witches' from *Oh How Silly*, published by Methuen
Ian Serraillier for 'Andrew's Bedtime Story', from *Happily Ever After*, published by Oxford University Press
William Jay Smith for 'Things'
The Society of Authors as the literary representative of the Estate of Rose Fyleman for 'Mice'
Mrs. A. M. Walsh for 'Taking Out Jim' by John Walsh

The Red Herring

There was once a high wall, a bare wall. And
against this wall, there was a ladder,
a long ladder. And on the ground,
under the ladder, there was a red
herring. A dry red herring.

And then a man came along. And in his hands
(they were dirty hands) this man had
a heavy hammer, a long nail
(it was also a sharp nail) and
a ball of string. A thick ball of string.

All right. So the man climbed up
the ladder (right up to the top)
and knocked in the sharp nail:
spluk! Just like that.
Right on top of the wall. The bare wall.

Then he dropped the hammer. It dropped
right down to the ground. And onto the nail
he tied a piece of string, a long
piece of string, and onto the string
he tied the red herring. The dry red herring.

And let it drop. And then he climbed
down the ladder (right down
to the bottom), picked up the hammer
and also the ladder (which was pretty heavy)
and went off. A long way off.

And since then, that red herring, the dry
red herring on the end of the string, which is
quite a long piece, has been
very very slowly swinging and
swinging to a stop. A full stop.

I expect you wonder why I made
up this story, such a simple story. Well,
I did it just to annoy people.
Serious people. And perhaps also
to amuse children. Small children.

George Macbeth

The Beaver

The beaver is fat,
and his tail is so flat
that it closely resembles an oar.
He's known for his teeth,
those on top and beneath,
and he lives just a trifle off shore.

He nibbles on trees
as a mouse nibbles cheese
with incisors as sharp as a knife.
And with dexterous tricks
builds a house out of sticks
for his children, himself, and his wife.

Jack Prelutsky

Trace these lines on to a piece of paper, then join them up to make a very familiar animal.

Mice

I think mice
Are rather nice.

Their tails are long,
Their faces small,
They haven't any
Chins at all.
Their ears are pink,
Their teeth are white,
They run about
The house at night.
They nibble things
They shouldn't touch
And no one seems
To like them much.

But I think mice
Are nice.

Rose Fyleman

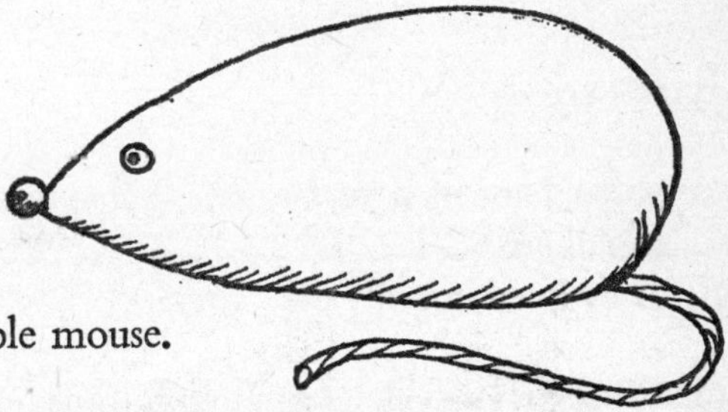

Make a . . .

pebble mouse.

Find a nice smooth pebble that has a flat bottom and is narrower at one end than the other. Using a very strong glue, stick a piece of string or a shoe-lace to the wider end, as a tail. Stick a tiny little pebble at the other end, to look like a nose, and paint on two bright eyes.

Now you might like to try to make other pebble animals. Here are some to keep your mouse company.

Mouse-charm against whooping cough

Get three field mice, flaw them, draw them and roast one of them and let the party affected eat it; dry the other two in the oven until they crumble to a powder, and put a little of this powder in what the patient drinks at night and in the morning.

Some people say that fleas are black,
But I know it isn't so;
For Mary had a little lamb
Whose fleas was white as snow.

Ridiculous Riddles

Q. What happened to the two kangaroos that had a spring wedding?
A. They lived hoppily ever after.

Q. What do you call a camel with three humps?
A. Humphrey.

Q. What happened to the budgie when the lawn mower ran over it?
A. It turned into shredded tweet.

The Six Badgers

As I was a-hoeing, a-hoeing my lands
Six badgers came up with white wands in their hands.
They made a ring around me and, bowing, they said:
'Hurry home, Farmer George, for the table is spread!
There's pie in the oven, there's beef on the plate:
Hurry home, Farmer George, if you would not be late!'
So homeward I went, but could not understand
Why six fine dog-badgers with white wands in hand
Should seek me out hoeing and bow in a ring,
And all to inform me so common a thing!

Robert Graves

Have You Ever Seen?

Have you ever seen A BAT?
Flitting-flying, sky-diving, brown-skinned,
Ears-listening.

Have you ever seen A CAT?
Slowly-stalking, prey-hunting, eyes-flashing,
Tail-swishing.

Have you ever seen A FOX?
Bushy-tailed, sly-thinking, rusty-colour,
Ever-hungry.

Have you ever seen A SPIDER?
Creeping-crawling, deep-black, legs-sprawling,
Shudder-shivering.

Have you ever seen A PHEASANT?
Long-tailed, brightly-coloured, proud-looking,
Stepping-neat.

Have you ever seen A DEER?
Spotted-back, lightly-walking, swiftly-shy,
Gentle-eyed.

K. Lampard (12 years old)

There was an old lady of Harrow
Who rode a large hamster to Jarrow,
Where they swam in the sea
And ate fishcakes for tea;
Then she wheeled him right home in a barrow.

Criss-cross Riddles

What do you get if you cross:

Q. A chirping insect with a flying mouse?
A. A cricket bat.

Q. A library with a maggot?
A. A bookworm.

Q. A hedgehog with a goat?
A. A stuck-up kid.

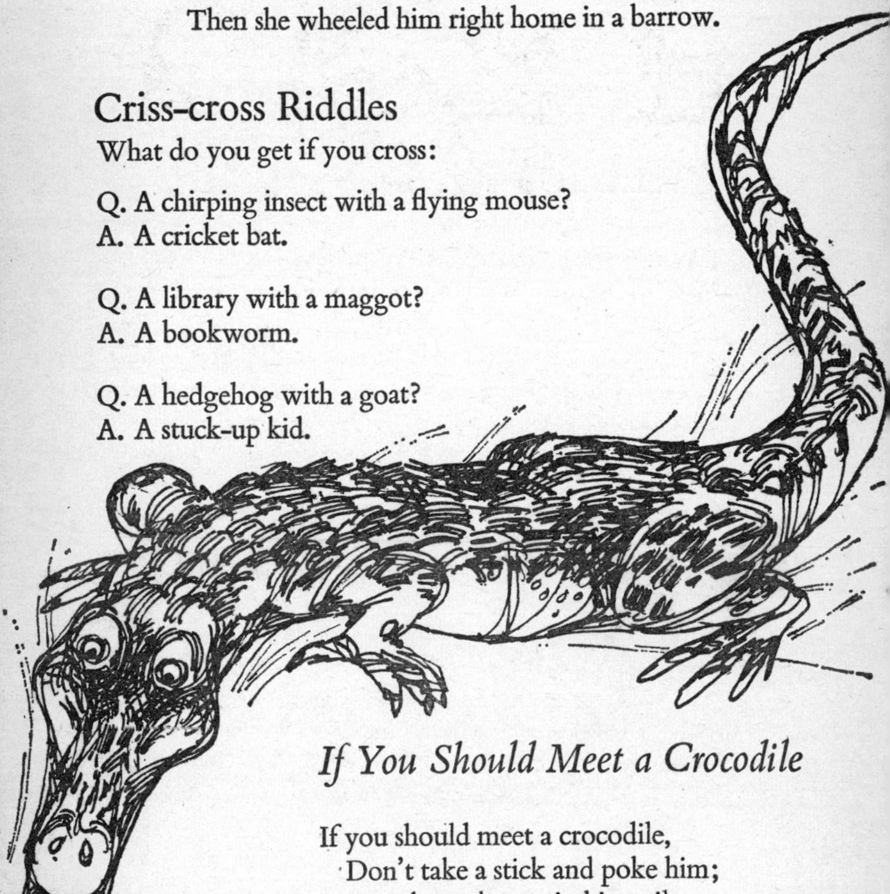

If You Should Meet a Crocodile

If you should meet a crocodile,
  Don't take a stick and poke him;
Ignore the welcome in his smile,
  Be careful not to stroke him.
For as he sleeps upon the Nile,
  He thinner gets and thinner;
And when e'er you meet a crocodile
  He's ready for his dinner.

Make a hungry crocodile

You will need:
a piece of card
a paper fastener
crayons or felt pens

This is what you do:
Trace the crocodile, and the crocodile's jaw from this page on to the card, colour them and cut them out.
Make the holes where they are marked on both pieces, and fix them together with the paper fastener so that the jaw can move.

If you wish to live and thrive
Let the spider go alive.

A Trunk-ful of Elephants

Q. Why were the elephants the last to leave the ark?
A. They had to pack their trunks.

Q. Why are elephants wrinkled all over?
A. Have *you* ever tried to iron one?

Q. Why do elephants wear sandals?
A. To stop them sinking in the sand.

Q. Why do ostriches hide their heads in the sand?
A. To look for the elephants who forgot to wear their sandals.

Q. What do you use to shoot an elephant?
A. A gun.

Q. Yes, an elephant gun. What do you use to shoot a pink elephant?
A. A pink elephant gun.

Q. Right. So what do you use to shoot a green elephant?
A. A green elephant gun.
Wrong. First you make the elephant blush, and then you use your pink elephant gun!

Q. Why do elephants paint their toe-nails cherry red?
A. So that they can hide in cherry trees.
Q. Why do elephants paint their toe-nails all sorts of colours?
A. So that they can hide in a box of all-sorts.

Q. Have you ever seen an elephant in a box of all-sorts?
A. No. Just shows what a good disguise it is!

Animals
(A game to play with a baby)

Here is the ostrich straight and tall,
Nodding his head above us all.
Stretch your arm above your head and stick your hand out, palm downwards.
Here is the long snake on the ground,
Wriggling upon the stones he found.
Stretch your arm straight out in front of you and wriggle your fingers.
Here are the birds that fly so high,
Spreading their wings across the sky.
Wave both your arms slowly up and down.
Here is the hedgehog, prickly, small,
Rolling himself into a ball.
Clench your fist.
Here is the spider scuttling round,
Treading so lightly on the ground.
Wiggle your fingers gently.
Here are the children fast asleep,
Pillow your head on your hands.
And here at night the owls do peep.
Make circles round your eyes with your thumb and first finger.

Kathleen Bartlett

Twist your tongue by saying this *very* quickly.

Swan, swim over the sea.
Swim, swan, swim!
Swan, swim back again.
Well swum, swan!

Fish tails

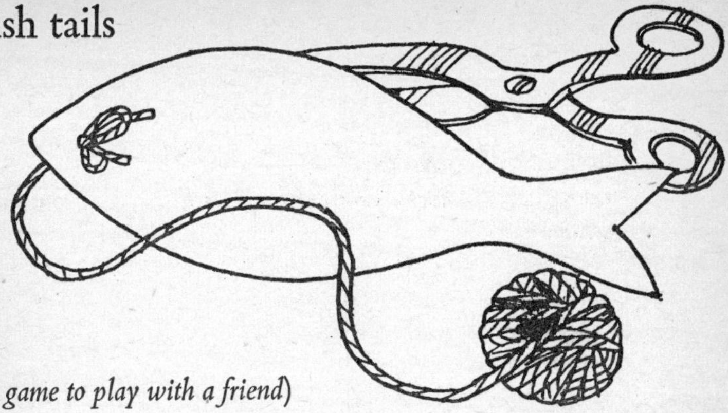

(A game to play with a friend)

Each player must cut out the shape of a fish – like this one but much bigger – from a piece of paper, and tie it on to a length of string. Fasten the string around your waist so that the fish can just lie flat on the ground behind you when you are standing up. Now, face your partner, count to three, and the game can begin. It's quite simple. Each one of you has to try to stamp on the other's fish, and the first one to manage it wins.

Go on playing for as long as you like. There's only one rule. You mustn't use your hands to push each other or twitch your fish tail, only to keep your balance.

Here are two eyes, and a curly tail. Trace them on to a clean sheet of paper, and then see what strange creature you can draw around them. Perhaps you'd like to make a whole zoo-ful of strange animals, and colour them with paints or crayons.

The rarest animal of all

Pushmi-pullyus are now extinct. That means, there aren't any any more. But long ago, when Doctor Dolittle was alive, there were some of them still left in the deepest jungles of Africa; and even then they were very, very scarce. They had no tail, but a head at each end, and sharp horns on each head. They were very shy and terribly hard to catch. The black men get most of their animals by sneaking up behind them while they are not looking. But you could not do this with the pushmi-pullyu – because, no matter which way you came towards him, he was always facing you. And besides, only one-half of him slept at a time. The other head was always awake – and watching. This was why they were never caught and never seen in Zoos. Though many of the greatest huntsmen and the cleverest menagerie-keepers spent years of their lives searching through the jungles in all weathers for pushmi-pullyus, not a single one had ever been caught. Even then, years ago, he was the only animal in the world with two heads.

Well, the monkeys set out hunting for this animal through the forest. And after they had gone a good many miles, one of them found peculiar footprints near the edge of a river; and they knew that a pushmi-pullyu must be very near that spot.

Then they went along the bank of the river a little way and they saw a place where the grass was high and thick; and they guessed that he was in there.

So they all joined hands and made a great circle round the high grass. The pushmi-pullyu heard them coming, and he tried hard to break through the ring of monkeys. But he couldn't do it. When he saw that it was no use trying to escape, he sat down and waited to see what they wanted.

They asked him if he would go with Doctor Dolittle and be put on show in the Land of the White Men.

But he shook both of his heads hard and said, 'Certainly not!'

They explained to him that he would not be shut up in a

menagerie but would just be looked at. They told him that the Doctor was a very kind man but hadn't any money; and people would pay to see a two-headed animal and the Doctor would get rich and could pay for the boat he had borrowed to come to Africa in.

But he answered, 'No. You know how shy I am – I hate being stared at.' And he almost began to cry.

Then for three days they tried to persuade him.

And at the end of the third day he said he would come with them and see what kind of a man the Doctor was, first.

So the monkeys travelled back with the pushmi-pullyu. And when they came to where the Doctor's little house of grass was, they knocked on the door.

'What in the world is it?' asked John Dolittle, gazing at the strange creature.

'This, Doctor,' said Chee-Chee, 'is the pushmi-pullyu – the rarest animal of the Africa jungles, the only two-headed beast in the world! Take him home with you and your fortune's made. People will pay any money to see him.'

'But I don't want any money,' said the Doctor.

'Yes, you do,' said Dab-Dab, the duck. 'Don't you remember how we had to pinch and scrape to pay the butcher's bill in Puddleby?'

'Well, perhaps there is something in what you say,' murmured the Doctor. 'It certainly would make a nice new kind of pet. But does the er- what-do-you-call-it really want to go abroad?'

'Yes, I'll go,' said the pushmi-pullyu, who saw at once, from the Doctor's face, that he was a man to be trusted. 'You have been so kind to the animals here – and the monkeys tell me that I am the only one who will do. But you must promise me that if I do not like it in the Land of the White Men you will send me back.'

'Why, certainly – of course, of course,' said the Doctor. 'Excuse me, surely you are related to the Deer Family, are you not?'

'Yes,' said the pushmi-pullyu – 'to the Abyssinian Gazelles and the Asiatic Chamois – on my mother's side. My father's great-grandfather was the last of the Unicorns.'

'Most interesting!' murmured the Doctor.

'I notice,' said the duck, 'that you only talk with one of your mouths. Can't the other head talk as well?'

'Oh yes,' said the pushmi-pullyu. 'But I keep the other mouth for eating – mostly. In that way I can talk while I'm eating without being rude. Our people have always been very polite.'

from The Story of Doctor Dolittle *by Hugh Lofting*

What, Why and When?

Q. What kind of animals didn't go into the Ark in pairs?
A. Worms. They went in in apples.

Q. Why did the lobster blush?
A. Because it saw the salad dressing.

Q. When is milk not milk?
A. When it's turned into a saucepan.

I Don't Suppose

I don't suppose
A lobster knows
The proper way
To blow his nose –
Or else perhaps
Beneath the seas
They have no need
To sniff and sneeze?

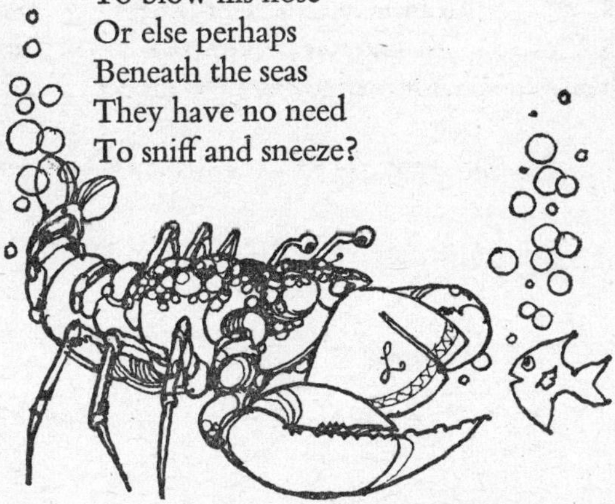

Hurt No Living Thing

Hurt no living thing,
Ladybird nor butterfly,
Nor moth with dusty wing,
Nor cricket chirping cheerily,
Nor grasshopper, so light of leap,
Nor dancing gnat,
Nor beetle fat,
Nor harmless worms that creep.

Christina Rossetti

The river bank

As the Mole sat on the grass and looked across the river, a dark hole in the bank opposite, just above the water's edge, caught his eye, and dreamily he fell to considering what a nice snug dwelling-place it would make for an animal with few wants and fond of a bijou riverside residence, above flood level and remote from noise and dust. As he gazed, something bright and small seemed to twinkle down in the heart of it, vanished, then twinkled once more like a tiny star. But it could hardly be a star in such an unlikely situation; and it was too glittering and small for a glow-worm. Then, as he looked, it winked at him, and so declared itself to be an eye; and a small face began gradually to grow up round it, like a frame round a picture.

A little brown face, with whiskers.

A grave round face, with the same twinkle in its eye that had first attracted his notice.

Small neat ears and thick silky hair.

It was the Water Rat!

Then the two animals stood and regarded each other cautiously.

'Hullo, Mole!' said the Water Rat.

'Hullo, Rat!' said the Mole.

'Would you like to come over?' inquired the Rat presently.

'Oh, it's all very well to *talk*,' said the Mole, rather pettishly, he being new to a river and riverside life and its ways.

The Rat said nothing, but stooped and unfastened a rope and hauled on it; then lightly stepped into a little boat which the Mole had not observed. It was painted blue outside and white within, and was just the size for two animals; and the Mole's whole heart went out to it at once, even though he did not yet fully understand its uses.

The Rat sculled smartly across and made fast. Then he held up his fore-paw as the Mole stepped gingerly down. 'Lean on that!' he said. 'Now then, step lively!' and the Mole to his surprise and rapture found himself actually seated in the stern of a real boat.

'This has been a wonderful day!' said he, as the Rat shoved off and took to the sculls again. 'Do you know, I've never been in a boat before in all my life.'

'What?' cried the Rat, open-mouthed: 'Never been in a – you never – well, I – what have you been doing, then?'

'Is it so nice as all that?' asked the Mole shyly, though he was quite prepared to believe it as he leant back in his seat and surveyed the cushions, the oars, the rowlocks, and all the fascinating fittings, and felt the boat sway lightly under him.

'Nice? It's the *only* thing,' said the Water Rat solemnly, as he leant forward for his stroke. 'Believe me, my young friend, there is *nothing* – absolutely nothing – half so much worth doing as simply messing about in boats. Simply messing,' he went on dreamily: 'messing – about – in boats; messing – '

'Look ahead, Rat!' cried the Mole suddenly.

It was too late. The boat struck the bank full tilt. The dreamer, the joyous oarsman, lay on his back at the bottom of the boat, his heels in the air.

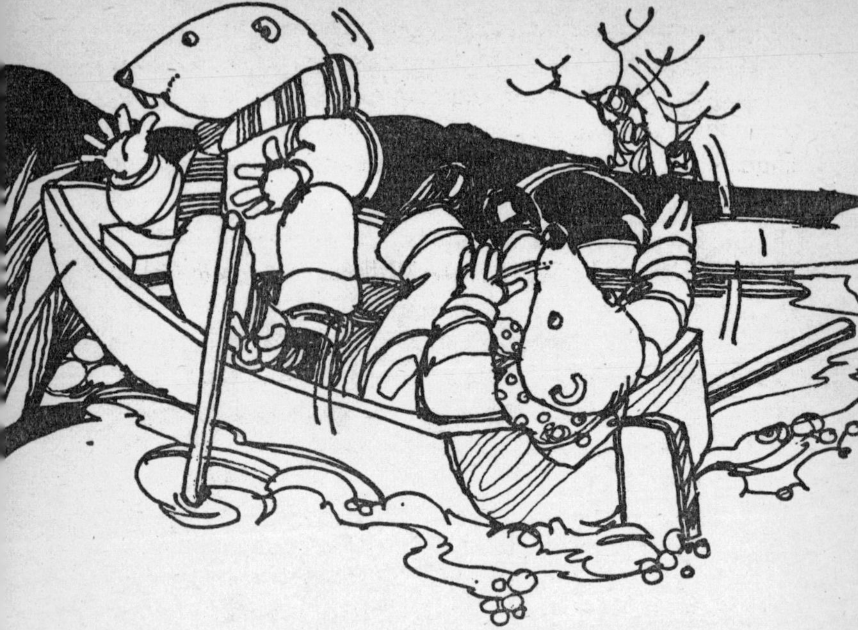

'– about in boats – or *with* boats,' the Rat went on composedly, picking himself up with a pleasant laugh. 'Look here! If you've really nothing else on hand this morning, supposing we drop down the river together, and have a long day of it?'

The Mole waggled his toes from sheer happiness, spread his chest with a sigh of full contentment, and leaned back blissfully into the soft cushions. '*What* a day I'm having!' he said. 'Let us start at once!'

'Hold hard a minute, then!' said the Rat. He looped the painter through a ring in his landing-stage, climbed up into his hole above, and after a short interval reappeared staggering under a fat, wicker luncheon-basket.

'Shove that under your feet,' he observed to the Mole, as he passed it down into the boat. Then he untied the painter and took the sculls again.

'What's inside it?' asked the Mole, wriggling with curiosity.

'There's cold chicken inside it,' replied the Rat briefly; 'coldtonguecoldhamcoldbeefpickledgherkinssaladfrenchrolls cress – sandwidgespottedmeatgingerbeerlemonadesodawater –'

'O stop, stop,' cried the Mole in ecstasies: 'This is too much!'

'Do you really think so?' inquired the Rat seriously. 'It's only what I always take on these little excursions; and the other animals are always telling me that I'm a mean beast and cut it *very* fine!'

from The Wind in the Willows *by Kenneth Grahame*

Sunshine food – three recipes for flower sandwiches

1 Rose petal sandwiches

You will need:
12 slices of thin bread
soft cream cheese
butter
strawberry jam
fresh rose petals that you have washed and dried

This is what you do:
Butter six slices of bread and spread the other six with cheese. Spread a layer of jam on top of the cheese, and a layer of petals on top of the jam. Put a slice of buttered bread on top of the petals, then cut each sandwich into fingers.

2 Marigold canapés

You will need:

4 slices of brown bread, buttered
2 hard-boiled eggs
1 heaped tablespoon of mayonnaise or salad cream
1 level dessertspoonful of sweet pickle
salt
fresh marigold petals

This is what you do:

Chop the hard-boiled eggs in a bowl and add mayonnaise or salad cream, salt and sweet pickle. Spread the mixture thickly on to the bread, then cut each slice into four triangles. Now sprinkle bright marigold petals over the top.

3 Nasturtium sandwiches

You will need:

6 slices of white bread
6 slices of whole wheat bread
butter
mayonnaise or salad cream for spreading
½ cup of chopped-up chicken or tuna fish
¼ cup of chopped-up celery
an extra ¼ cup of mayonnaise for mixing
salt and pepper
nasturtium petals and leaves

This is what you do:

Spread the white bread with butter, and the wheat bread with mayonnaise. Mix together the chicken or tuna, celery, ¼ cup of mayonnaise and about a dozen chopped-up nasturtium leaves. Spread this mixture on to the slices of whole wheat bread. Cover with a layer of nasturtium petals, letting them stick out round the edges to make a colourful frill, then put the slices of white bread on to the top, and cut into neat squares.

Suppertime

The room in which the boys were fed was a large stone hall, with a copper at one end, out of which the master, dressed in an apron for the purpose, and assisted by one or two women, ladled the gruel at meal-times. Of this festive composition each boy had one porringer, and no more – except on occasions of great public rejoicing, when he had two ounces and a quarter of bread besides. The bowls never wanted washing. The boys polished them with their spoons till they shone again; and when they had performed this operation (which never took very long, the spoons being nearly as large as the bowls), they would sit staring at the copper with such eager eyes as if they could have devoured the very bricks of which it was composed, employing themselves, meanwhile, in sucking their fingers most assiduously, with the view of catching up any stray splashes of gruel that might have been cast thereon. Boys have generally excellent appetites. Oliver Twist and his companions suffered the tortures of slow starvation for three months; at last they got so voracious and wild with hunger that one boy, who was tall for his age, and hadn't been used to that sort of thing (for his father had kept a small cook-shop), hinted darkly to his companions that unless he had another basin of gruel each day, he was afraid he might some night happen to eat the boy who slept next him, who happened to be a weakly youth of tender age. He had a wild, hungry eye, and they implicitly believed him. A council was held; lots were cast who should walk up to the master after supper that evening and ask for more; and it fell to Oliver Twist.

The evening arrived; the boys took their places. The master, in his cook's uniform, stationed himself at the copper; his pauper assistants ranged themselves behind him; the gruel was served out, and a long grace was said over the short commons. The gruel disappeared; the boys whispered each other, and winked at Oliver, while his next neighbours nudged him. Child as he was, he was desperate with hunger, and reckless with misery. He rose from the table, and advancing to the master, basin and spoon

in hand, said, somewhat alarmed at his own temerity:

'Please, sir, I want some more.'

The master was a fat, healthy man, but he turned very pale. He gazed in stupefied astonishment on the small rebel for some seconds, and then clung for support to the copper. The assistants were paralysed with wonder, the boys with fear.

'What!' said the master at length, in a faint voice.

'Please, sir,' replied Oliver, 'I want some more.'

The master aimed a blow at Oliver's head with the ladle, pinioned him in his arms, and shrieked aloud for the beadle.

from Oliver Twist *by Charles Dickens*

Advice to a Cannibal

(from a suggestion by Lewis Carroll)

Never stew your sister
You'll be sorry when you've missed her,
For there's no fun in cooking
Anyone who is looking
Something like yourself.

Never bake your brother
He's so much like your mother
And they'll both be very bitter
If you eat him in a fritter
At a midnight barbecue.

Never fry your father –
There'd be a great palaver,
And he'd come and haunt you nightly
And bring you indigestion
Like an undigested question.

Never grill your grandad,
Although he was a bad lad,
You'll need a steady nerve
To pepper, salt and serve
Your chief and royal ancestor.

Whatever's on the menu,
Make sure it's never *you*.
Try to stay uneaten,
And avoid becoming beaten
In an omelette or soufflé.

Kenneth Agar

Cannibal Quips

1st Cannibal: 'I don't know what to make of my husband these days!'
2nd Cannibal: 'How about a hot-pot?'

A cannibal chief of Penzance
Ate an uncle and two of his aunts,
And then a large piece
Of a rather fat niece,
And now he can't button his pants.

Deedle deedle dumpling, my son John,
Ate a pasty five feet long;
He bit it once, he bit it twice,
He found that it was full of mice!

Limericks

There was an old man of Dumbree,
Who taught little owls to drink tea;
For he said, 'To eat mice
Is not proper or nice,'
That amiable man of Dumbree.

There was an old person of Dean
Who dined on one pea, and one bean;
For he said, 'More than that
Would make me too fat,'
That cautious old person of Dean.

Edward Lear

Greedy Dog

This dog will eat anything.

Apple cores and bacon fat,
Milk you poured out for the cat.
He likes the string that ties the roast
And relishes hot, buttered toast.
Hide your chocolates! He's a thief,
He'll even eat your handkerchief.
And if you don't like sudden shocks,
Carefully conceal your socks.
Leave some soup without a lid,
And you'll wish you never did.
When you think he must be full,
You find him gobbling bits of wool,
Orange peel or paper bags,
Dusters and old cleaning rags.

This dog will eat anything,
Except for mushrooms and cucumber.

Now what is wrong with those, I wonder?

James Hurley

Vegetable animals

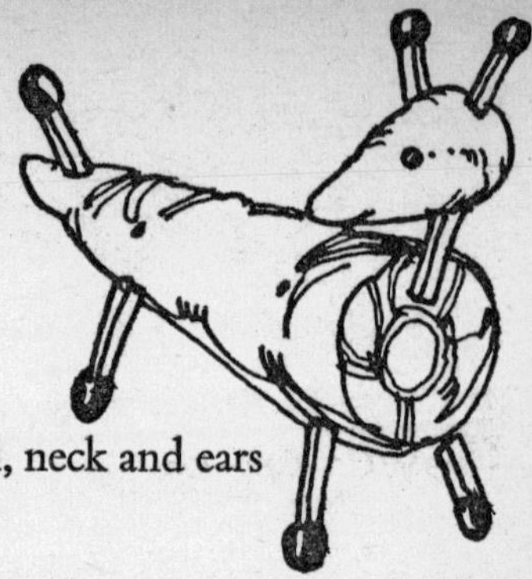

Make DOUGLAS the DACHSUND

You will need:
a long thin carrot for his body
8 short sticks to make his legs, tail, neck and ears
plasticine for his head

This is what you do:
Cut off the top of the carrot – you won't need this.
Make a dog's pointed head with plasticine, and fix this on to the neck stick.
Push two tiny sticks into the top of it as ears.
Push four sticks into the carrot-body, to make the legs.
Push the neck and head into position in the piece of carrot that you have cut.
As a last touch, put a little stick in the back end, as his tail.

Make HECTOR the HEDGEHOG

You will need:
a potato for his body
used matches or wooden cocktail sticks for his spines
four lolly sticks for his legs

This is what you do:
Cut the bottom of the potato, if necessary, so that it is flat.
Leaving a space at the front for a face, push spines all over the body.
Push the legs into position beneath it.

Tongue-Twister

Lally licks lollies lolling lazily.

Flower-cubes

This is a pleasant idea which will delight your friends, and is quite simple to prepare.

You will need:
edible flowers – rose petals, violets, marigolds, nasturtium, wisteria are all possible – carefully washed
the ice-making tray of the fridge, filled with clean cold water

This is what you do:
simply put one little flower, or petal, into each square of the tray, then put it into the ice-making compartment to freeze. When the cubes have frozen each will have a little flower visible inside, and they will look very pretty floating about in your friends' cold drinks.

The Boa Constrictor

I'm being swallowed by a boa constrictor, a boa constrictor, a boa constrictor,
I'm being swallowed by a boa constrictor,
And I don't like it one bit.

Oh no! It's up to my toe.
Oh gee! It's up to my knee.
Oh fiddle! It's up to my middle.
Oh heck! It's up to my neck.
Oh dread! It's up to my . . . GULP.

Poor Algy

Algy met the bear,
The bear met Algy,
The bear was bulgy,
The bulge was Algy.

Another Tongue Twister . . .

Tuesday is stew day. Stew day is Tuesday.

. . . And another

For sheep soup, shoot sheep.

Tommy – a game to play with sweets

You will need:
one or two friends to play with, and a packet of candy-covered chocolate buttons

This is what you do:
Spread seven sweets on the table. Choose one person to have the first go, and ask him to shut his eyes tight while the rest of you decide which sweet will be 'Tommy'. Then he must open his eyes and begin to pick up and eat the sweets one by one. But as soon as he touches Tommy the rest of you shout 'TOMMY', and his turn is finished. Now someone else can try his luck. While he sits with his eyes closed the number of sweets is made up to seven once more and the game begins again. It will finish when you have eaten all the sweets.

Deborah Delora

Deborah Delora, she liked a bit of fun –
She went to the baker's and bought a penny bun;
Dipped the bun in treacle and threw it at her teacher –
Deborah Delora! What a wicked creature!

How Quickly Can You Say It?

'Miss Cissy Smith dismisseth us.'

A B C D E F G
Little Robin Redbreast sitting on a tree;
H I J K L M N
He made love to little Jenny Wren;
O P Q R S T U
Dear little Jenny, I want to marry you;
V W X Y Z
Poor little Jenny, she blushed quite red.

Two Ns, three As, an S and a B –
What do you think that this can be?

This should give you a clue. Trace it on to a piece of paper, then finish the drawing.

The ABC

'Twas midnight in the schoolroom
And every desk was shut,
When suddenly from the alphabet
Was heard a loud 'Tut-tut!'

Said A to B, 'I don't like C;
His manners are a lack.
For all I ever see of C
Is a semicircular back!'

'I disagree,' said D to B,
'I've never found C so.
From where *I* stand, he seems to be
An uncompleted O'.

C was vexed. 'I'm much perplexed,
You criticise my shape.
I'm made like that, to help spell Cat
And Cow and Cool and Cape.'

'He's right,' said E; said F, 'Whoopee!'
Said G, ' 'Ip, 'ip, 'ooray!'
'You're dropping me,' roared H to G.
'Don't do it please, I pray!'

'Out of my way,' LL said to K.
'I'll make poor I look ILL.'
To stop this stunt, J stood in front,
And presto! ILL was JILL.

'U know,' said V, 'that W
Is twice the age of me,
For as a Roman V is five
I'm half as young as he.'

X and Y yawned sleepily,
'Look at the time!' they said.
They all jumped in to beddy byes
And the last one in was Z!

Spike Milligan

First lessons

That same summer Edwin's mother began to teach him to read. He had had books of his own for a long time and often thought how it would be when they began to talk too. Then the letters turned into animals, birds and all kinds of things and soon they began to go about together two and two: A stood about under a tree called B, and C came and did the same, but when three or four of them got together they began to quarrel with each other and nothing went right. And the further he went on the less he remembered who they all were; the one that stayed longest in his head was A because he liked him best, but soon he forgot him too and there were no stories left in the book but only lessons.

One day his mother came in and said to him, 'School begins again tomorrow and you must go up to the farm.'

Edwin had heard that a school was a place a lot of boys played about in, and he had nothing against that. He was very pleased at the idea. He had often been to the farm but never when the school was there, and he walked faster than his mother up the hill in his eagerness to be there. As they reached the old people's house a great rumbling came out of it like the sound of the mill at home and he asked his mother what it was.

'It's the children reading,' she answered and he was very glad to hear it, for that was just how he had read before he learned his letters. When he went in, there were more children sitting there round a table than he had ever seen in church; others were sitting on their satchels against the walls and some stood in knots round a blackboard; the schoolmaster, an old man with grey hair, sat on a stool near the fireplace filling his pipe. When Edwin and his mother came in, everyone looked up and the rumble of the mill stopped as if the sluice of the mill stream had been shut down.

'I have brought you a little boy who wants to learn to read,' said his mother

'What is the little chap's name?' said the schoolmaster, groping

into his pouch for more tobacco.

'Edwin,' said his mother. 'He knows his letters and he can spell.'

'Can he now?' said the schoolmaster. 'Come here to me then.'

Edwin went over to him and the schoolmaster caught him up, put him on his knee and took his cap off.

'You're a fine fellow,' he said.

Edwin looked him straight in the eye and laughed.

'Are you laughing at me?' he asked, frowning.

'Yes, I am,' replied Edwin and burst out laughing again. Then the schoolmaster laughed too, and his mother laughed and the children all felt they could laugh too so they all laughed together. That was how Edwin came to school.

from A Norwegian Childhood *by Bjornsterne Bjornsen, translated by George Elvey and taken from* A Golden Land

Make a secret code wheel

You will need:
a breakfast plate
a saucer
card
paper
a paper fastener
a ruler
a protractor
a pencil
scissors

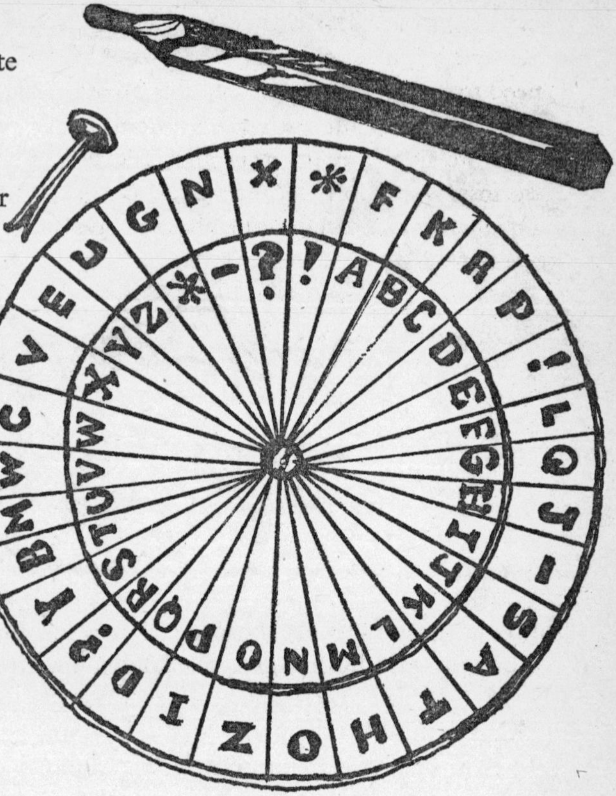

This is what you do:
Lay a sheet of paper over the card, and a plate face down on top, and draw a circle round it. Cut around the pencilled line so that you have two identical circles, one of card, and one of paper then repeat the process with the saucer. Now fold each paper, circle in half, twice, pressing down the folds so that when you open them out there is a clear cross. Lay the paper circle on top of their matching card circles, and pierce a hole through the points where the lines cross. Now throw away the paper circles, lay the

smaller card circle on top of the larger one, and fasten them together through the centre with a paper fastener, so that they can be moved around.

Mark off the double disc into thirty equal sections. (You may need to use a protractor to do this, making each section 12°. If you find it difficult, ask a grown-up to help.)

Write all the letters of the alphabet, in their correct order, in the inside circle, and fill the four spaces that are left with * – ? !. On the outside circle write the alphabet and these four signs again, but this time they must all be jumbled up.

Now, start your code where you see the * on the inside circle. That sign, with the letter opposite in the outside circle, makes your *vital clue*. To make a message, you work out the letters you want on the inside circle, and write down the letters you find opposite them on the outside circle. Give an identical code wheel to your friend and he will be able to read your message. All he needs to do is to line up the vital clue properly, then he will be able to work out the letters. Every time you send a message turn the central disc so that the vital clue will change and the code will be different.

Here's a message for you, worked out from the Secret Code Wheel on this page. Can you work it out?

*UJT*HP*LPDFP*MPDDP*RPDX

A Number Puzzle

Think of any number from 1 to 9.
Multiply it by 3.
Add 1.
Multiply it by 3 again.
Add the number you first thought of.
Now you have the answer. You'll find that it ends with 3. If you remove the 3 you are left with the number you first thought of. Try it on your friends – you'll find it always works.

Jargon

Jerusalem, Joppa, Jericho –
These are the cities of long ago.

Jasper, jacinth, jet and jade –
Of such are jewels for ladies made.

Juniper's green and jasmine's white,
Sweet jonquil is spring's delight.

Joseph, Jeremy, Jennifer, James,
Julian, Juliet – just names.

January, July and June –
Birthday late or birthday soon.

Jacket, jersey, jerkin, jeans –
What's the wear for sweet sixteens?

Jaguar, jackal, jumbo, jay –
Came to dinner, but couldn't stay.

Jellies, junkets, jumbals, jam –
Mix them up for sweet-toothed Sam.

To jig, to jaunt, to jostle, to jest –
These are the things that Jack loves best.

Jazz, jamboree, jubilee, joke –
The jolliest words you ever spoke.

From A to Z and Z to A
The joyfullest letter of all is J.

James Reeves

How Many Miles?

How many miles to Old Norfolk
To see a magician breathe fire and smoke?
1, 2, 3, 4,
Only 3 miles more.
How many miles to Christmas Cove
To eat an applecake baked with clove?
1, 2, 3, 4,
Only 2 miles more.
How many miles to Newburyport
For trinkets and sweets of every sort?
1, 2, 3, 4,
Only 1 mile more.
How many miles to Lavender Spring
To hear a fine trumpeter play for the king?
1, 2, 3, 4,
Here we are, we'll go no more.

Clyde Watson

Eight Magpies

I saw eight magpies in a tree,
Two for you and six for me:
One for sorrow, two for mirth,
Three for a wedding, four for a birth:
Five for England, six for France,
Seven for a fiddler, eight for a dance.

Ten Little Chickens

Ten little chickens went out to dine,
One got lost – and then there were nine.

Nine little chickens went through a gate,
One got jammed – and then there were eight.

Eight little chickens went walking in Devon,
One ran away – and then there were seven.

Seven little chickens went picking up sticks,
One ran home again – and then there were six.

Six little chickens went for a dive,
One swam away – and then there were five.

Five little chickens went knocking on the door,
One wouldn't go inside – and then there were four.

Four little chickens chased a bumble bee,
One got stung – and then there were three.

Three little chickens went off to the zoo,
One stayed behind – and then there were two.

Two little chickens broke into a run,
One got short of breath – and then there was one.

One little chicken went walking in the sun,
And he forgot to go home – so now there are none.

The Dove and the Wren

The dove says, 'Coo
What shall I do?
It's hard, so hard, to keep my two.'

'Pooh', says the wren,
'Look, I've got ten
And keep them all like gentlemen.'

Magic Square Puzzle

Copy this square on to a piece of paper. You'll see that only three of the boxes are filled. You fill the others with the figures 0, 1, 2, 3, 4, 5, so that each row, across, up and down and corner to corner, adds up to 12.

Cottage

When I live in a Cottage
I shall keep in my Cottage

Two different Dogs
Three creamy Cows
Four giddy Goats
Five Pewter Pots
Six silver Spoons
Seven busy Beehives
Eight ancient Appletrees
Nine red Rosebushes
Ten teeming Teapots
Eleven chirping Chickens
Twelve cosy Cats with their kittenish Kittens and
One blessed Baby in a Basket.

That's what I'll have when I live in my Cottage.

Eleanor Farjeon

Skipping Song

One I love, two I loathe,
Three I cast away;
Four I love with all my heart,
Five I love, I *say*.
Six he loves me, seven he don't,
Eight he'll marry me, nine he won't,
Ten he would if he could, but he can't,
Eleven he comes, twelve he tarries,
Thirteen he's waiting, fourteen he marries.

Country Counting

aina
peina
para
peddera
pimp
ithy
mithy
owera
lowera
dig
ain-a-dig
pein-a-dig
par-a-dig
pedder-a-dig
bumfit
ain-a-bumfit
pein-a-bumfit
par-a-bumfit
pedder-a-bumfit
giggy

A Lot of ...

a chatter of teeth
a theft of magpies
a snap of hypnotists
a tetley of tea-bags
a lick of lollipops
a black eye of boxers
a fire of dragons
a mist of flies
a night of witches
a tinker of cars
a parachute of jellyfish
a snap of alligators
a blind of options

These descriptions for 'lots of things' were made up by children aged from eight to eleven. Perhaps you'd like to make up some of your own? What word would you choose to describe a lot of:

children

butterflies

aunties

handkerchiefs

worms

teachers

sugar lumps

clowns

dentists

Make an advent-box

You will need:
25 matchboxes, all the same size
glue
card
coloured sticky paper
scissors

This is what you do:
Glue the boxes on top of each other in piles of five so that you have five little chests of drawers. Now stand the chests side by side and glue the sides together.

Cut a long strip of card so that it is the exact size needed to fit snugly around the sides and across the top of the set of boxes. Fold it neatly at the corners, and glue it into place.

Decorate the card with colourful cut-out shapes, and put bright figures on the fronts of the drawers, numbering them from 1 to 25, in any order you choose.

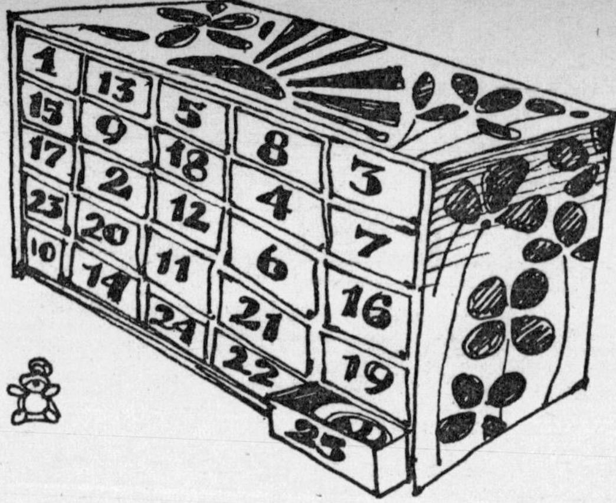

Put a tiny gift into each drawer – a wrapped sweet, a ring, beads, pretty buttons, an eraser, a pair of dice, a sugar lump, for example – and give the Advent Box to a friend. He will be able to open one drawer every day from December 1st until Christmas Day. You'll probably like to put the nicest gift of all into the drawer marked 25.

Our Family

Sue works in a shop. John's driving a bus,
Joan's married to Frank and is not living with us,
Tom wants to leave school as soon as he can,
Father still speaks like a West Countryman;
So that's all of us, with Mother and me,
In our family.

Crystella's from Cyprus, George, Port of Spain,
His father talks cricket and works on a crane,
Lynn, born in Jamaica, is slender and tall,
Fazi wears earrings and comes from Bengal;
So that's some of them, their mothers, and me,
In our family.

Leonard Clark

Grandpa Tom

Among the earliest, and happiest, memories of my childhood are my country walks with Grandpa Tom.

Grandpa Tom was always called by his Christian name so I wouldn't get him mixed up with the other old man in my life, Grandpa Jim, but I must admit that to my child's mind this need for distinction was always a mystery. How could anyone possibly mistake one for the other? While Grandpa Jim was a tiny, gentle, timid creature, with soft, silvery hair and an apologetic smile, Grandpa Tom was a lion among men.

He stood six feet four in his socks, and boasted a vast, billowing stomach that filled me with amazed incredulity. Could it really be all him? Iron-grey hair bristled over his head, erupted into extraordinary eyebrows, and sprouted, extravagantly, from his ears. He had the strength of an ox, the bellow of a bull . . . and an infinite tenderness for little children and wild flowers.

Grandpa Tom was, by profession, a chemist, and in those days that meant a herbalist too. He used the flowers and fruits of the countryside for a huge variety of purposes. He'd make rose hip syrup for a winter tonic, fragrant pot pourri to freshen a sick room, herbal tobacco for the relief of asthma and bronchitis. From the hedgerows he'd find the ingredients for moth and insecticide powders, pain-killers, laxatives, sedatives, hair rinses and skin lotions. And when he was away from his dispensary he'd conjure up a whole range of delectable wines, jams, jellies, soups and casseroles, banishing Grandma from the kitchen while he hung over his bubbling pots and aromatic stew pans.

Just now and then, when the season was right and the weather smiled on us, Grandpa Tom would take me with him on one of his collecting expeditions. He'd cram his ancient trilby firmly down over his ears, grab his walking stick in one hand and me in the other, and together we'd set off along the flowering lanes in search of treasure.

They still grow there, the flowers I loved, but strangely, they all seem to have shrunk slightly. Then I wandered among blossomy forests of foaming meadowsweet and Queen Anne's lace, stood on tip-toe to watch a bee disappear with triumphant buzz into the spotted velvet of a foxglove bell, measured my height against the purple and gold of willowherb and buttercup.

Gradually, I learned where to look for the treasures – where to find the first sweet white violets, where the bluebells were bluest, the marsh marigolds most magnificent. The flowers were my first alphabet; I learned their country names, their flowering seasons, the folk lore and legend that surrounded them. It was a long and loving apprenticeship, and with Grandpa Tom as my master, I was an apt pupil.

A family portrait gallery

You can make shadow pictures of your favourite people.

You will need:
a torch
some large sheets of black paper and some large sheets of white paper, all the same size
drawing pins or blu-tack
pencil
scissors
glue

This is what you do:
Prop up the torch so that it shines on a wall and fasten up a piece of white paper where the light shines most brightly.

Ask a friend to sit sideways in front of the paper so that his head throws a shadow on it, then draw around the outline.

Now cut round the drawing so that you make a hole in the paper the exact shape of your friend's head.

Glue the white paper on to the black paper to make a black and white cameo portrait. You can frame it if you wish by making a neat edging of coloured sticky tape.

Ridiculous Riddles

Q. Why are granny's teeth like stars?
A. Because they come out at night.

Q. Why did the silly boy put his father in the refrigerator?
A. Because he wanted ice-cold pop.

Q. Which is bigger, Mrs Bigger or Mrs Bigger's baby?
A. Mrs Bigger's baby is just a little Bigger.

A Very Odd Fish

(D'Arcy Wentworth Thompson, who wrote this poem, was an Edinburgh schoolmaster one hundred years ago. His young wife died after the birth of their son and so the little boy was brought up by his grandmother who insisted that he should be given his father's name, 'D'Arcy Wentworth'. Not surprisingly, he was quite unable to pronounce 'D'Arcy' so he called himself 'Dadu' and this is the name his father uses in this poem he wrote about him.

Little Dadu must have enjoyed rambling on the shore with his father and granny because when he grew up he became a distinguished marine biologist.)

Granny and I with dear Dadu,
Went rambling on the shore;
With pebbles smooth and cockleshells
We filled his pinafore.

Beneath the stones and in the pool
We found, to our delight,
Shrimps, periwinkles, and a most
Voracious appetite.

Grandma's Pajamas

A sleeper from the Amazon
Put nighties of his gra'mazon –
  The reason: that
  He was too fat
To get his own pajamazon.

Family holiday

The summer holidays were well advanced when we were told we were going with Father and Mother to stay at a farmhouse in Kent. We had been to the seaside several times, but had never been to the real country before, and Cyril and I were very excited at the prospect. I asked innumerable questions. The farm was called Pollard's.

'Mother, what is it like? Do they have cows?'

'Yes, darling, I expect there will be lots of cows, and we shall get nice fresh farmhouse butter.'

'But, Mother, the Dorset butter we have at home is salt and I don't like it.'

'Well, I'm sure the butter will be nice, and you'll have eggs all new laid, and perhaps home-made bread.'

'Ooh!' was all I could say to that. Then – 'Mother, do they have rabbits as well as cocks and hens?'

'I expect so, and pigs as well, and they say there are hop fields, and if we stay long enough we can see them picking the hops. It is great fun; all the families in the neighbourhood come, children and all, and pick away all day. When Uncle Henry was Rector of Chiddingstone I stayed with them and we all went picking, and I remember how sore it made my fingers.'

It was afternoon when we climbed into the train at Charing Cross. Cyril and I always enjoyed a railway journey, though it was a pity we were not allowed to lean out of the windows. After stopping at a number of stations, we began to leave behind the little houses and chimneys of the outskirts of London and the afternoon sun shone on fields and lanes. Before we reached our destination Father pointed out some hop fields. The hops were trained up poles, and Father explained how the poles were laid across canvas bags for the picking.

Pollard's Farm was several miles from the station, and the porter who handled our luggage told us that the farm wagonette was waiting for us. There, sure enough, it was, with a youth, whom the porter called Charlie, standing by the horse's head.

The luggage was piled on, and off we started. It had begun to rain a little, so Cyril and I, sitting on the box-seat, spread a tarpaulin cape over our shoulders.

As we went along, Charlie told us about the farm. He told us of a new litter of pigs, for one thing, and how Mrs Pollard had won a prize for bread at the village Show. It was all very new and exciting, especially when we came in sight of some queer-shaped, pointed roofs. 'They be oast houses,' Charlie told us, pointing with his whip, 'where they dry and pocket the hops. Like enough you'll see them doin' it – that is, if you're here at the right time.'

The road was getting muddy and the horse splashed in the puddles as we trotted along. Soon we turned into a narrow lane and saw ahead of us a red-tiled farmhouse. 'Pollard's,' said Charlie. At the end of the lane we passed through an open gate,

and drove round to the back of the square-fronted farmhouse, pulling up in a spacious yard. A black and white rough-haired dog came out of his kennel with much rattling of his chain, and stood barking and waving his tail.

The farmhouse door was opened and a woman came out. She was very stout, with a cheerful red face. She greeted us in a friendly way, but when Father and Mother shook hands with her she was rather flustered. Wiping her hands on her apron first, she said, ''Tis the flour, with me baking buns for the young people.' Cyril and I exchanged a quick look. 'Buns!'

We went in through a great kitchen where a small maid was trying to hide behind an enormous deal table. She bobbed a curtsey, and stood looking at us with her mouth open. Charlie carried in our luggage, and Cyril and I were sent upstairs to wash.

There was no bathroom, but washstands with white china jugs and basins were in the bedrooms, which were pervaded by a faint smell of camphor. We boys had a large room, the floor of which sloped, so that we felt we were going downhill when we went to the window. This had white dimity curtains. The bed, which we were to share, was very large and very soft to bounce on; there was a feather mattress in which we could feel the spikes of the feathers, when we pressed it, but it proved rather hot to sleep in. Below the window was a small, neat garden, and by looking sideways we could see into the farmyard with its tiled roofs, and beyond could glimpse a wooden barn and some haystacks.

It did not take us long to wash and we ran along to have a look at Ethel's room. It was gayer than ours, with a spotted pink wallpaper and bright curtains, but was very small and grown-ups had to duck their heads under the doorway.

Lovely smells were now coming up from below as of sizzling bacon and eggs, and we clattered downstairs to the parlour, which was not often used but now was brushed up for the occasion. We were greeted by a delectable sight. The round table fairly groaned under the weight of good things. Plates loaded with buns, pots of jam, a dish of yellow butter and a large plum cake. Then there was a great round loaf, and plates of biscuits and cheese, and bottles of pickles, and in fact everything you could think of. A great brown teapot was standing on a side table. Our eyes were goggling at it all when Mrs Pollard came in with a dish full of bacon and eggs. She said proudly, ' 'Tis home-cured, and I hope it will be enough.' Even Father's eyes sparkled and we boys hardly knew where to begin.

When the feast came to an end, and we had stuffed till we could stuff no more, Cyril and I lay back in our chairs. We had planned to explore the farm, but overcome by drowsiness, decided to let that wait till tomorrow; anyhow it was growing dark. A lamp was brought in. Outside, the rain had stopped and there were distant farmyard sounds. It was all very peaceful. As I sat there a large moth flew in at the window and began to flutter round and round the lamp. I grew sleepier and sleepier. Father was reading the newspaper, and he looked up and said, 'Those boys ought to be in bed.' As this was exactly what I had been thinking, we went upstairs to our feather-bed without a murmur, and only Mother's reminder saved us from going to sleep without cleaning our teeth or saying our prayers.

from Drawn from Memory *by Ernest H. Shepard*

The Stern Parent

Father heard his Children scream,
So he threw them in the stream,
Saying, as he drowned the third,
'Children should be seen, *not* heard!'

Harry Graham

My Uncle Paul of Pimlico

My Uncle Paul of Pimlico
Has seven cats as white as snow,
Who sit at his enormous feet
And watch him, as a special treat
Play the piano upside down,
In his delightful dressing gown;
The firelight leaps, the parlour glows,
And, while the music ebbs and flows,
They smile (while purring the refrains),
At little thoughts that cross their brains.

Mervyn Peake

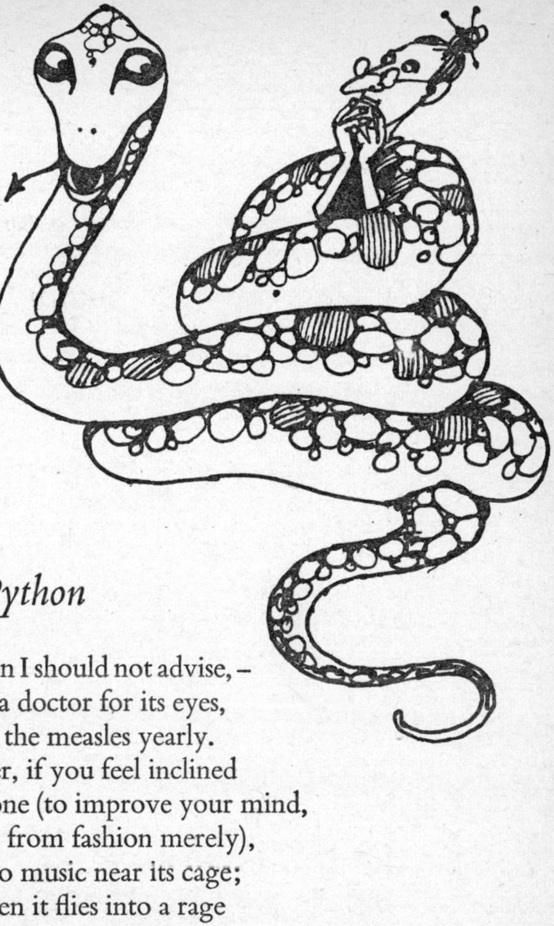

The Python

A Python I should not advise, –
It needs a doctor for its eyes,
And has the measles yearly.
However, if you feel inclined
To get one (to improve your mind,
And not from fashion merely),
Allow no music near its cage;
And when it flies into a rage
Chastise it, most severely.
I had an Aunt in Yucatan
Who bought a Python from a man
And kept it for a pet.
She died, because she never knew
These simple little rules and few; –
The snake is living yet.

Hilaire Belloc

Make a family mobile

You will need:
4 or 5 cardboard cylinders from toilet paper and kitchen paper rolls
card
glue
felt-tip pens
a wire coat-hanger
a needle
strong thread
scissors
wool and paper scraps

This is what you do:
Cut the cardboard rolls so that they are all different sizes, and draw on them faces and clothes, so that they look like little people. You might like to stick wool on for hair, and attach little paper legs to the bottom of each roll.

Cut a circle of card big enough to fit over the top of each cylinder. Thread your needle with a length of cotton and make a large knot in the end, then take the cotton through the centre of the first card circle and fasten the unknotted end to the bar of the coat hanger. Fasten hanging threads to all your circles in this way so that they hang from the bar without touching each other.

Spread strong glue around the top rim of each cylinder and stick to the underside of each circle. When the glue is quite set you can hang up your little family and watch them gently floating and circling in space.

Manners at Table when away from Home

(These lines of advice were written five hundred years ago, when it was common for boys of about seven or eight to be sent away from home to live in a great man's house. There they would learn not only how to read and write, but also the polite customs and manners of their time.)

Little children, here ye may lere,
Much courtesy that is written here.
Look thine hands be washen clean,
That no filth in thy nails be seen.
Take thou no meat till grace be said
And till thou see all things arrayed.
Look, my son, that thou not sit
Till the ruler of the house thee bid.
And at thy meat, in the beginning,
Look on poor men that thou think:
For the full stomach ever fails
To understand what the hungry ails.
Eat not thy meat too hastily,
Abide and eat easily.
Carve not thy bread too thin,
Nor break it not in twain:
The morsels that thou beginnest to touch
Cast them not in thy pouch.
Put not thy fingers in thy dish,
Neither in flesh, neither in fish;
Put not thy meat in to the salt
(Into thy cellar that thy salt halt)
But lay it fair on thy trencher
Before thee, that is honour.

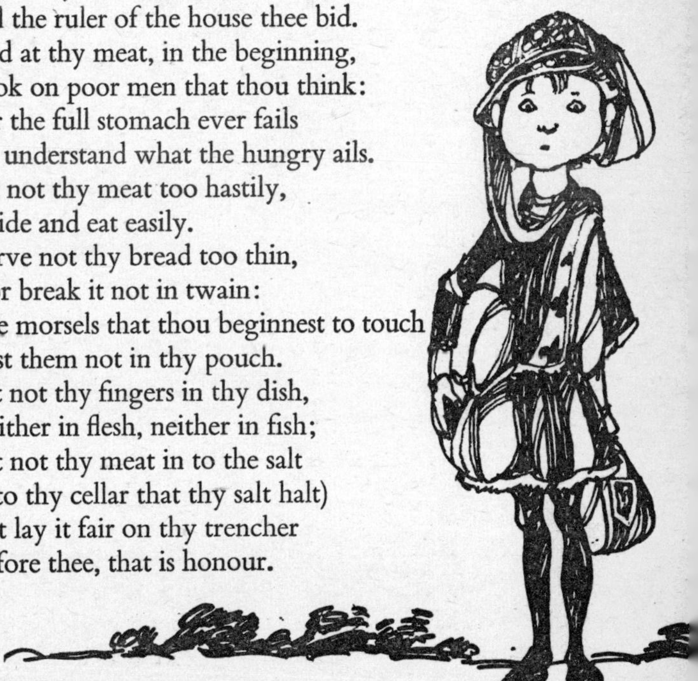

Pick not thine ears nor thy nostrils,
If thou do, men will say thou com'st of churls.
And while thy meat in thy mouth is
Drink thou not – forget not this.
Eat thy meat by small morsels,
Fill not thy mouth as doeth rascals.
Pick not thy teeth with thy knife;
In no company begin thou strife.
And when thou hast thy pottage done,
Out of thy dish put thou thy spoon.
Nor spit thou not over the table
Nor thereupon – for it is not able.
Lay not thine elbow nor thy fist
Upon the table whilst thou eat'st.
Bulk not, as a bean were in thy throat,
As a churl that comes out of a cot.
And if thy meat be of great price
Be ware of it, or thou art not wise.

Bite not thy meat, but carve it clean:
Be well ware no drop be seen.
When thou eatest gape not too wide,
That thy mouth be seen on every side.
And son, be ware, I rede, of one thing,
Blow neither in thy meat nor in thy drink.

And cast not thy bones unto the floor,
But lay them fair on thy trencher.
Keep clean thy cloth before all
And sit thou still, whatso befall,
Till grace be said unto the end,
And till thou have washen with thy friend.
And spit not in thy basin,
My sweet son, that thou washest in;
And arise up soft and still,
And jangle neither with Jack nor Jill,
But take thy leave of thy host lowly,
And thank him with thine heart highly.
Then men will say thereafter
That 'A gentleman was here'.

Taking Out Jim

We left the dusty
Road and wheeled
The push-chair straight
Into the field;
So thick the dande-
lions grew;
We thought we'd deck
The baby too.

So standing in
A circle round him,
With Linda's straw
School-hat we crowned him;
Stuck dandelions
Round the band,
And squeezed a big one
In his hand.

With dandelion-
Chains a-swinging,
We sang his praise
In softest singing;
We called him Dande-
lion Jim,
And pelted him,
And tickled him.
Half-smothered under
Linda's hat,
All giggling
And plump he sat,
A pollen-patch
Upon his nose,
And juice-stains down
His new white blouse.

Then, overcome
By sudden fears,
We brushed the petals
From his ears,
Straightened his hair
With Beryl's comb,
And thought we'd better
Take him home.

John Walsh

Finger Families

(*A finger game*)

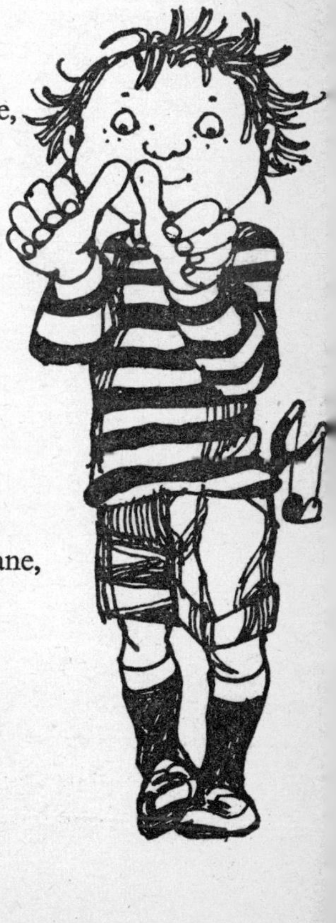

Two portly Grandpapas met down the lane,
(*bring your thumbs together*)
Bowed so politely, bowed once again,
How de do, how de do, how de do again.
Two dainty aunties met down the lane,
(*forefingers*)
Curtseyed politely, curtseyed again,
How de do, how de do, how de do again.
Two tall uncles met down the lane,
(*middle fingers*)
Shook hands politely, shook hands again,
How de do, how de do, how de do again.
Two grinning schoolboys met down the lane,
(*fourth fingers*)
Nodded politely, nodded again,
How de do, how de do, how de do again.
Two chuckling babies met down the lane,
(*little fingers*)
Gurgled politely, gurgled again,
How de do, how de do, how de do again.

Fingerling puppets

You can make a whole family of little people for finger-play games.

For each puppet you will need:
2 pieces of felt, about 75 mm square
paper
a pencil
scissors
adhesive
pins
scraps of material,
wool, buttons, etc.

This is what you do:
Draw the outline of a man, woman or child on your paper, making it big enough to fit over your finger, but not too big for your material. Cut round this shape and you have made your paper pattern.

Lay your pattern on the two pieces of felt, placed one on top of the other, and pin it into place. Now cut round the outline, and remove the pins.

Glue the edges of the two pieces of felt together, except for the bottom edge which you must leave open so that your finger can fit inside.

When the glue is quite dry make a face on your puppet with scraps of felt and give him hair made from strands of wool.

Your fingerling puppet is now complete unless you want to dress it with some tiny buttons, a frilly collar, a hat, or a tie made from scraps of material.

Wart meets Merlyn

There was a clearing in the forest, and in this clearing there was a snug little cottage built of stone. It was a cottage, although the Wart did not notice this at the time, which was divided into two bits. The main bit was the hall or every-purpose room, which was high because it extended from floor to roof, and this room had a fire on the floor whose smoke issued eventually out of a hole in the thatch of the roof. The other half of the cottage was divided into two rooms by a horizontal floor which made the top half into a bedroom and study, while the bottom half served for a larder, store room, stable and barn. A white donkey lived in this downstairs room, and a ladder led to the one upstairs.

There was a well in front of the cottage, and the metallic noise which the Wart had heard was caused by a very old gentleman who was drawing water out of it by means of a handle and chain.

Clank, clank, clank, said the chain, until the bucket hit the lip of the well, and 'Oh, drat the whole thing,' said the old gentleman. 'You would think that after all these years of study one could do better for oneself than a by-our-lady well with a by-our-lady bucket, whatever the by-our-lady cost.'

'I wish to goodness,' added the old gentleman, heaving his bucket out of the well with a malevolent glance, 'that I was only on the electric light and company's water, drat it.'

The old gentleman that the Wart saw was a singular spectacle. He was dressed in a flowing gown with fur tippets which had the signs of the zodiac embroidered all over it, together with various cabalistic signs, as of triangles with eyes in them, queer crosses, leaves of trees, bones and birds and animals and a planetarium whose stars shone like bits of looking glass with the sun on them. He had a pointed hat like a dunce's cap, or like the headgear worn by ladies of the time, except that the ladies were accustomed to have a bit of veil floating from the top of it. He also had a wand of lignum vitae, which he had laid down in the

grass beside him, and a pair of horn-rimmed spectacles like those of King Pellinore. They were extraordinary spectacles, being without ear pieces, but shaped rather like scissors or the antennae of the tarantula wasp.

'Excuse me, sir,' said the Wart, 'but can you tell me the way to Sir Ector's castle, if you don't mind?'

The aged gentleman put down his bucket and looked at the Wart. 'Your name would be Wart,' he said.

'Yes, sir, please, sir,' said the Wart.

'My name,' said the aged gentleman, 'is Merlyn.'

'How do you do?' said the Wart.

'How do you do?' said Merlyn. 'It is clement weather, is it not?'

'It is,' said the Wart, 'for the time of the year.'

When these formalities had been concluded, the Wart had leisure to examine his new acquaintance more closely. The aged gentleman was staring at him with a kind of unwinking and benevolent curiosity which made him feel that it would not be rude at all to stare back, no ruder than it would be to stare at one of his guardian's cows who happened to be ruminating his personality as she leaned her head over a gate.

Merlyn had a long white beard and long white moustache which hung down on either side of it, and close inspection showed that he was far from clean. It was not that he had dirty finger-nails or anything like that, but some large bird seemed to have been nesting in his hair. The Wart was familiar with the nests of the spar-hawk and the Gos, those crazy conglomerations of sticks and oddments which had been taken over from squirrels and crows, and he knew how the twigs and the tree foot were splashed with white mutes, old bones, muddy feathers and castings. This was the impression that he gained from Merlyn. The old gentleman was streaked with droppings over his shoulders, among the stars and triangles of his gown, and a large spider was slowly lowering itself from the tip of his hat, as he gazed and slowly blinked at the little boy in front of him.

from The Sword In The Stone *by T. H. White*

My Cats
(a witch speaks)

I like to toss him up and down
A heavy cat weighs half a crown
With a hey do diddle my cat Brown.

I like to pinch him on the sly
Whcn nobody is passing by
With a hey do diddle my cat Fry.

I like to ruffle up his pride
And watch him skip and turn aside
With a hey do diddle my cat Hyde.

Hey Brown and Fry and Hyde my cats
That sit on tombstones for your mats.

Stevie Smith

Which wicked witch is the weird wizard's whacky widow?

Mother Bumby's charm against witchcraft

Gather the herb pimpernell, saying while it is gathered:

'Herbe pimpernell, I have thee found
Growing upon Christ Jesus' ground:
The same gifte the Lord Jesus gave unto thee,
When He shed His blood upon the tree.
Arise up, pimpernell, and go with me,
And God bless me,
And all that shall weare thee. Amen.'

Say this fifteen days together, twice a day, morning early fasting, and in the evening full.

Witch-words ...

Trefoil, Johnswort, Vervain and Dill,
Hinder witches of their will.

To Make Sure That No Dog Will Bite you place a leaf of the herb Hound's Tongue in your shoe beneath your big toe.

... and warnings

Do not burn the wood of the elder. If you do, the Devil will come down the chimney.

Never eat blackberries after the end of September. On the first of October, the Devil spits on them.

Make a thumb-ghost

You will need:
a black, felt-tipped pen
a large, white handkerchief

This is what you do:
The pad of your thumb is to be the ghost's face. Draw on it two large black ghostly eyes, and a large ghostly mouth, wide open so that it looks as if it is wailing.

Drape the handkerchief over the top of your thumb and around your hand – and you are ready to make your ghost haunt your friends. He looks most effective popping up from the edge of a table.

Johnny Dow

Who lies here?
I, Johnny Dow.
Who! Johnny is that you?
Aye, man, but I'm dead now.

Some Say

Some say the deil's deid,
The deil's deid, the deil's deid,
Some say the deil's deid,
An' buried in Kirkcaldy.

Some say he'll rise again,
Rise again, rise again,
Some say he'll rise again,
An' dance the Hielan Laddie.

Make your own magic

A magic garden

Put some lumps of coal, or an old broken brick, into a large shallow dish.

Mix together:
1 spoonful of ammonia
$\frac{1}{4}$ cupful of salt
$\frac{1}{4}$ cupful of water with washing 'blue' dissolved in it.
$\frac{1}{4}$ cupful of plain water
coloured ink
(Warning – ammonia is a rather strong and smelly chemical so treat it very carefully.)

Pour this mixture over the coal or brick, and put the dish into a warm place. Soon, shining crystals will begin to sparkle in the bowl. To keep your 'garden' growing, add another spoonful of ammonia once a week.

Magic buttons

Fill a tumbler with lemonade, and drop a small plastic button into it. After a while, the button will start to rise slowly to the top, and then, once it reaches the top, will fall to the bottom again. Add more buttons if you want to; they will also rise and fall slowly. The buttons will continue to bounce for about a quarter of an hour, until the lemonade loses its 'fizz.' (If you haven't any lemonade add some vinegar to a tumbler of water. This will not work as well but it does 'fizz' for a while.)

From Flannan Isle

'Though three men dwelt on Flannan Isle
To keep the lamp alight,
As we steered under the lee, we caught
No glimmer through the night.'
A passing ship at dawn had brought
The news; and quickly we set sail,
To find out what strange thing might ail
The keepers of the deep-sea light.
As we neared the lonely Isle,
And looked up at the naked height,
We saw the lighthouse towering white,
With blinded lantern, that all night
Had never shot a spark
Of comfort through the dark.
And as into the tiny creek
We stole beneath the hanging crag,
We saw three queer, black ugly birds –
Too big, by far, in my belief,
For cormorant or shag –
Like seamen sitting bolt-upright
Upon a half-tide reef:
But, as we neared, they plunged from sight,
Without a sound, or spurt of white.
And still too mazed to speak,
We landed; and made fast the boat;
And climbed the track in single file,
Each wishing he were safe afloat,
On any sea, however far,
So it be far from Flannan Isle.
Yet, all too soon, we reached the door,
The black, sun-blistered lighthouse-door,
That gaped for us ajar.
Yet, as we crowded through the door,
We only saw a table, spread

For dinner, meat and cheese and bread;
But, all untouched; and no one there:
As though, when they sat down to eat,
Ere they could even taste,
Alarm had come; and they in haste
Had risen and left the bread and meat:
For at the table-head a chair
Lay tumbled on the floor.

* * *

Ay: though we hunted high and low,
And hunted everywhere,
Of the three men's fate we found no trace
Of any kind in any place,
But a door ajar, and an untouched meal,
And an overtoppled chair.
And as we listened in the gloom
Of that forsaken living-room –
A chill clutch on our breath –
We thought how ill-chance came to all
Who kept the Flannan Light:
And how the rock had been the death
Of many a likely lad:
How six had come to a sudden end,
And three had gone stark mad:
And one whom we'd all known as a friend
Had leapt from the lantern one still night,
And fallen dead by the lighthouse wall:
And long we thought
On the three we sought,
And of what might yet befall.
We seemed to stand for an endless while,
Though still no word was said,
Three men alive on Flannan Isle,
Who thought on three men dead.

Wilfred Wilson Gibson

King Charles the First walked and talked half an hour after his head was chopped off.

How? – No, he wasn't a ghost. Just add one piece of punctuation and you will understand.

Playground ghost story

In a dark, dark wood, there was a dark, dark house,
And in that dark, dark house, there was a dark, dark room,
And in that dark, dark room, there was a dark, dark cupboard,
And in that dark, dark cupboard, there was a dark, dark shelf,
And in that dark, dark shelf, there was a dark, dark box,
And in that dark, dark box, there was a *GHOST*!

Two's Company

(The sad story of the man who didn't believe in ghosts.)

They said the house was haunted, but
He laughed at them and said, 'Tut, tut!
I've never heard such tittle-tattle
As ghosts that groan and chains that rattle;
And just to prove I'm in the right,
Please leave me here to spend the night.'
They winked absurdly, tried to smother
Their ignorant laughter, nudged each other,
And left him just as dusk was falling
With a hunchback moon and screech-owls calling –
Not that this troubled him one bit;
In fact, he was quite glad of it,
Knowing it's every sane man's mission
To contradict all superstition.
But what is that? Outside it seemed
As if chains rattled, someone screamed!
Come come, it's merely nerves, he's certain
(But just the same, he draws the curtain),
The stroke of twelve – but there's no clock!
He shuts the door and turns the lock.
(Of course, he knows that no one's there,
But no harm's done by taking care!);
Someone's outside – the silly joker,
(He may as well pick up the poker!)
That noise again! He checks the doors,
Shutters the windows, makes a pause
To seek the safest place to hide –
(The cupboard's strong – he creeps inside).
'Not that there's anything to fear,'
He tells himself, when at his ear
A voice breathes softly, 'How do you do!
I am the ghost. Pray, who are you?'

Raymond Wilson

Flower-charm to conjure fairies

Now must ye gather and pluck, when the sun is at his highest point, those flowers that fairies do choose, as rag-wort, rye-grass, freckled fox-glove, bluebell and pale primrose.

Find out those trees that fairies most frequent, as hawthorn, elder and the oak, and at that time of the month when the moon is full, strew the ground beneath withal, saying as ye go:

'Herbs and grasses here I bring,
Dance within thy fairy ring,
Grace be with me in this hour,
Shield me from thy fairy power.'

Children's Fairy-ring Song

In and out the dusky bluebells,
In and out the dusky bluebells,
In and out the dusky bluebells,
I am your master.

Tipper-ipper-apper on your shoulder,
Tipper-ipper-apper on your shoulder,
Tipper-ipper-apper on your shoulder.
I am your master.

The fairy queen holds court

Titania, the Fairy Queen: I'll give thee fairies to attend on thee,
And they shall fetch thee jewels from the deep,
And sing, while thou on pressed flowers dost sleep:
And I will purge thy mortal grossness so
That thou shalt like an airy spirit go.
Pease-blossom! Cobweb! Moth! and Mustardseed!
Pease-blossom: Ready.
Cobweb: And I.
Moth: And I.
Mustardseed: And I.
All Four: Where shall we go?
Titania: Be kind and courteous to this gentleman;
Hop in his walks, and gambol in his eyes;
Feed him with apricocks and dewberries,
With purple grapes, green figs, and mulberries.
The honey-bags steal from the humble-bees,
And for night-tapers crop their waxen thighs,
And light them at the fiery glow-worm's eyes,
To have my love to bed, and to arise;
And pluck the wings from painted butterflies
To fan the moonbeams from his sleeping eyes:
Nod to him, elves, and do him courtesies.

from A Midsummer Night's Dream *by*
William Shakespeare

Theseus and the Minotaur

The terms of the peace could only be described as harsh. Minos, king of Crete, having declared war on Athens to revenge the death of his son there, had defeated the city. Now, fourteen young Athenians – seven young men and seven young women – must be sent to Crete each year, to be sacrificed to the Minotaur.

The Minotaur was a hideous monster, half man and half bull. Nobody knew where it came from. It was kept in a labyrinth that Minos had had built specially, a complicated maze of rooms and tunnels, all underground. Once inside, it was impossible to find your way out of it again.

Every year, those Athenian parents whose families were of the right age had to take part in a lottery. They went to the Market Square and took a small ball from a sack. If the ball was black, they had to send their child to Crete.

This had been going on for several years when Theseus, the prince of Athens, came home, having finished his education in another country. When he arrived, the lottery was being held, and the city was in mourning. Sadly, his father explained what had happened.

'But why do the people go? Why don't they refuse?' Theseus asked.

'Minos would only send another army,' his father replied wearily. 'The lottery is less trouble than another war.'

'Then someone should try to kill the Minotaur. That would stop the sacrifice.'

'How could the beast be killed?' his father retorted. 'It is huge and fearsome, a man-eater. And no-one is allowed to take a weapon into the labyrinth. Besides, even if someone did manage to kill it, how would he find his way out again?'

'No matter. It *must* be done. I shall go myself.'

At length Aegeus realised that his son was absolutely determined, and reluctantly agreed to the plan. Theseus set sail with the others, for Crete.

Once the ship had arrived, the victims were presented

to Minos in his palace. At once Theseus announced himself as the son of Aegeus, noble prince of Athens, and asked that he should be allowed to go into the labyrinth first. Minos granted his wish, but Ariadne, Minos' daughter, decided that she must somehow try to save the life of this handsome young man.

That night she went down to the prison in which the Athenians were being kept to see him.

'Theseus,' she whispered, 'I have bribed the guards. Hurry to your ship and sail back to Athens. But take me with you or my father will kill me.'

'No,' said Theseus, 'I came here to kill the Minotaur. I cannot leave until I have done it.'

'Then let me help you.'

Gladly, Theseus agreed. The next evening, as he prepared to go into the labyrinth, Ariadne handed him a weapon. 'Here is my first gift, a silver sword. I have dipped the end in poison.' Theseus took the sword and hid it inside his shirt. 'But you will still have to find your way out again. Here is my second gift, a ball of string. Take this with you, but make sure you tie one end to the big rock that stands at the entrance to the maze.'

Theseus thanked her and marched bravely to the labyrinth. The guards set him on his way, then turned to leave him. ''Ave a nice time, mate,' one of them said.

And he was on his own; himself, his sword, and his ball of string against the monster.

The search to find the beast took a long time. The architect who built the place had done his job thoroughly. Eventually, though, he caught sight of it, every bit as huge and hideous as his father had said, lying at the far end of a narrow cavern. He stopped. By way of an answer, the Minotaur put his head down and charged. Theseus quickly stepped out of its way into a dark hollow in the walls. Bending down quietly, he picked up a stone and threw it a little distance. In the darkness the Minotaur thought that Theseus was standing where the noise had come from. Furiously, it charged again. As it raced past, Theseus stepped out and sank his sword into the beast's chest. It died quickly. 'Strong stuff, that poison,' Theseus thought.

When he came out of the labyrinth, after following the ball of string back through its long, winding tunnels, he found Ariadne waiting for him by the entrance. Together, they hurried to the prison, released the young Athenians, and led them down to their ship in the harbour. The crew was astonished to see them, but it did not take them long to set their sails and leave the unhappy island of Crete.

Andrew's Bedtime Story

I told him a tale that I adore
Called Theseus and the Minotaur,
Of how a prince with a ball of wool
  That his girl friend Ariadne gave him,
Was forced to search for a fiery bull
  Through cave and labyrinth. Keen to save him,
She said, 'Unwind the wool as you go
Through the twisting corridors down below,
And return to me safe – I love you so.'

That was the start of the tale I told,
And Andrew listened, as good as gold.
Next day when he ran home from school,
He found a skein of his mother's wool,
Unwound it, tied it to door and chair,
Along the passage and up the stair,
  Yes, everywhere.
I opened the door of my room
  To find
Pitschi the cat with his legs entwined,
Jane and Helen flat on the floor,
Great-aunt almost sliced at the knees

(As wire at the grocer's slices cheese),
All of them trapped.
The thread I snapped,
With scissors and knife I hacked away
And set them free.
But where was A?
There, in a corner lurking, laughing.
'No more
Of Ariadne's thread,
My boy,' I cried, 'or we'll all be dead!'
I stalked away.
But a murderous thread not seen before
Tripped me up, and I cracked my head.

Ian Serraillier

Prayer

No exorciser harm thee!
Nor no witchcraft charm thee!
Ghost unlaid forbear thee!
Nothing ill come near thee!

The monster and the prince

This is an exciting tracking game for two players, to be played where there are plenty of bushes and trees, or other things to hide behind. To start with, both of you must make a headband from string and paper, with a password written on it so that it can be seen both from the front and from behind. Don't let anyone see you writing your password – this must be kept a secret until the game is won.

Each player should find himself a den, and each den should have some 'treasure' in it – a cardboard box would do perfectly well. At the beginning of the game both players should know where both dens are and what the treasure looks like, and each one must be in his own den.

When the game begins, at a given signal, you must each put on your headband, then leave your den to try to do two things – to discover your enemy's password, *and* to steal his treasure. The winner is the first one to get the other's treasure back to his own den, and to shout out his opponent's password.

(Notice that you will need to think up new passwords each time you play this game.)

The carol singers

Bring out the tall tales now that we told
by the fire as the gas-light bubbled like a diver.
Ghosts whooed like owls in the long nights
when I dared not look over my shoulder; animals
lurked in the cubbyhole under the stairs where the
gas meter ticked. And I remember that we went
singing carols once, when there wasn't the shaving
of a moon to light the flying streets. At the end
of a long road was a drive that led to a large
house, and we stumbled up the darkness of the drive
that night, each one of us afraid, each one holding
a stone in his hand in case, and all of us too brave
to say a word. The wind through the trees
made noises as of old and unpleasant and maybe
web-footed men wheezing in caves. We reached
the black bulk of the house.
'What shall we give them? Hark the Herald?'
'No,' Jack said, 'Good King Wenceslas.
I'll count three.'
One, two three, and we began to sing,
our voices high and seemingly distant in the
snow-felted darkness round the house that
was occupied by nobody we knew. We stood
close together, near the dark door.
'Good King Wenceslas looked out
On the feast of Stephen. . . .'
And then a small, dry voice, like the voice
of someone who has not spoken for a long time,
joined our singing: a small, dry, egg-shell voice
from the other side of the door: a small, dry voice
through the keyhole. And when we stopped running
we were outside OUR house; the front room was lovely:
balloons floated under the hot-water-gulping gas;

everything was good again and shone over the town.
'Perhaps it was a ghost,' Jim said,
'Perhaps it was trolls,' Dan said,
who was always reading.

'Let's go in and see if there's any jelly left,'
Jack said. And we did that.

from Quite Early One Morning *by Dylan Thomas*

Whether the weather

Whether the weather be cold
Or whether the weather be hot
We'll weather the weather
Whatever the weather
Whether we like it or not.

From The Prelude

And in the frosty season, when the sun
Was set, and visible for many a mile
The cottage windows blazed through twilight gloom,
I heeded not their summons: happy time
It was indeed for all of us – for me
It was a time of rapture! Clear and loud
The village clock tolled six – I wheeled about,
Proud and exulting like an untired horse
That cares not for his home. All shod with steel,
We hissed along the polished ice in games
Confederate, imitative of the chase
And woodland pleasures – the resounding horn,

The pack loud chiming, and the hunted hare.
So through the darkness and the cold we flew,
And not a voice was idle.

William Wordsworth

Snowflakes

And did you know
That every flake of snow
That forms so high
In the grey winter sky
And falls so far
Is a bright six-pointed star?
Each crystal grows
A flower as perfect as a rose.
Lace could never make
The patterns of a flake
No brooch
Of figured silver could approach
Its delicate craftsmanship. And think:
Each pattern is distinct.
Of all the snowflakes floating there –
The million million in the air –
None is the same. Each star
Is newly forged, as faces are,
Shaped to its own design
Like yours and mine.
And yet . . . each one
Melts when its flight is done;
Holds frozen loveliness
A moment, even less;
Suspends itself in time –
And passes like a rhyme.

Clive Sansom

Making snowflakes

You will need:

a breakfast plate or saucer
pencil
scissors
clean white paper
thread
drawing pins

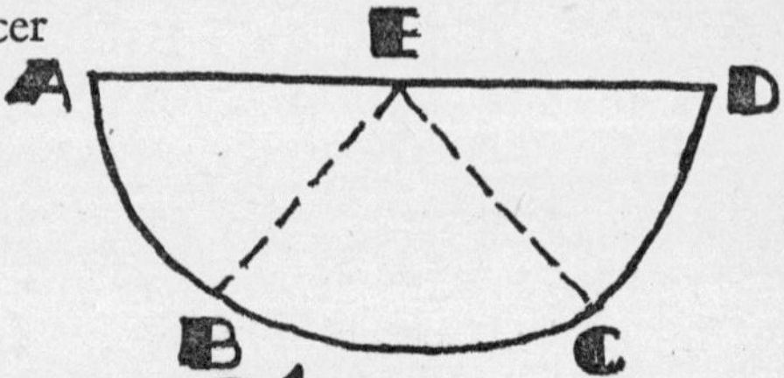

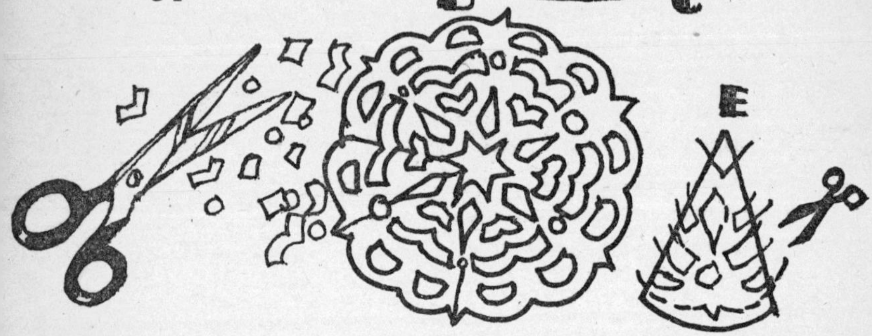

This is what you do:

On a plain white piece of paper draw a circle round the breakfast plate or saucer. Cut out the circle and fold it in half. Now you have a semi-circle. Fold this into three, as in the diagram, by folding A to C, and then D to B.

Now that you have a triangle shaped piece of paper, you can start cutting out your snowflake. Simply cut out shapes from the triangle, mainly around the three edges. When you have finished, unfold the triangle carefully – so as not to tear it – and you will find that whatever pattern you cut out is repeated six times in the finished snow flakes: 'a bright six-pointed star'.

If you cut the corner off (E), you will get a hole in the middle of your snowflakes. The more you cut out, the more intricate your snowflake will be. When you have finished, you can either hang the snowflake from the ceiling, using the thread and the drawing pin, or put them against the window. This looks even better if you cut them out in coloured crêpe paper.

The North Wind's winter recipe for the cold

Ingredients:

6 lbs of ice
5 lbs of snow
60 lbs of white trees
10 lbs of falling snow
3 lbs of frost
Bundle of snowballs
3 lbs of North Wind
Slides
Good handful of grey clouds.

Method:
Take the 5 lbs of snow and mix with the grey clouds and the wind. Add the white trees and drape half the ice on the trees. Take the bundle of snowballs and leave them by the slides, then put the rest of the ice on the slides. After this put the frost on the roads. When this is done, sprinkle the scene with the falling snow; then leave to set for three hours.

Anneliese Richter (11)

The Wind

Who has seen the wind?
  Neither I nor you;
But when the leaves hang trembling
  The wind is passing through.

Who has seen the wind?
  Neither you nor I;
But when the trees bow down their heads
  The wind is passing by.

Christina Rossetti

Three Traditional Riddles

White bird featherless
Flew from Paradise,
Pitched on the castle wall;
Along came Lord Landless,
Took it up handless,
And rode away horseless to the King's white hall.

A. Snow and sun

Purple, yellow, red and green,
The king cannot reach it,
No more can the queen.

A. A rainbow

There is a thing was three weeks old
When Adam was no more.
This thing it was but four weeks old
When Adam was four score.

A. The moon

Enjoy windy weather with a windmill

You will need:
a thin wooden stick, sharpened at one end
a cork
stiff coloured paper, 15 cms square
scissors
a pencil
a tumbler
a large pin
2 beads

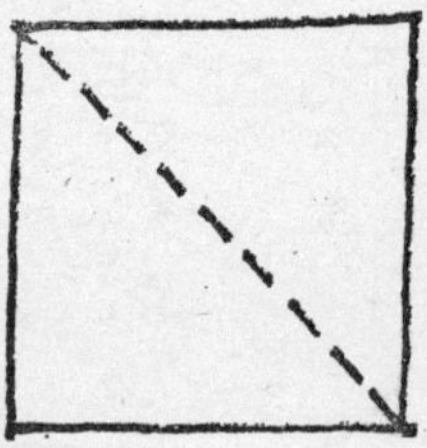

This is what you do:
1. Push the sharpened end of the stick into the side of the cork.

2. Find the centre of the square of paper by folding each corner inwards. Mark the central point where the corners meet.
3. Open the paper out again and place a tumbler upside down exactly over the central point. Draw a circle round the rim.
4. Cut the paper from each corner along the folded line as far as the circle.
5. Pierce a hole in the centre point, and in the right-hand corner of each section of the square, and then fold over each pierced corner until they meet together in the middle.
6. Put one bead on the pin, stick the pin through all the corner holes and then the central hole, and finish off with another bead.
7. Finally, push the pin firmly into the end of the cork, and your windmill is complete.

A Japanese flying fish kite

You will need:
3 pieces of coloured tissue paper, each about 30 cms wide and 60 cms long
a pencil
scissors
glue
crayons or felt-tipped pens
a short length of wire
strong thread
a long bamboo cane

This is what you do:
Lay two pieces of tissue paper one on top of the other, and draw the fish shape shown below on the upper one. Cut round the outline so that you have two identical shapes, then glue them together along the top and bottom.

When the glue is dry draw a large eye and some scales on both sides of the fish. From the third piece of tissue cut eight long streamers and stick them into position around the tail, then cut four short streamers and fasten two at either side of the fish's mouth, as gills.

Twist a piece of wire into a circle just the same size as the fish's mouth, put it inside the mouth, glue the inside of the tissue paper opening, and fold it back over the wire.

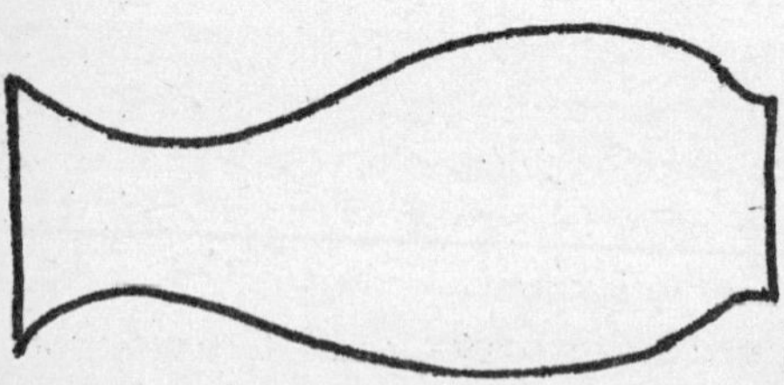

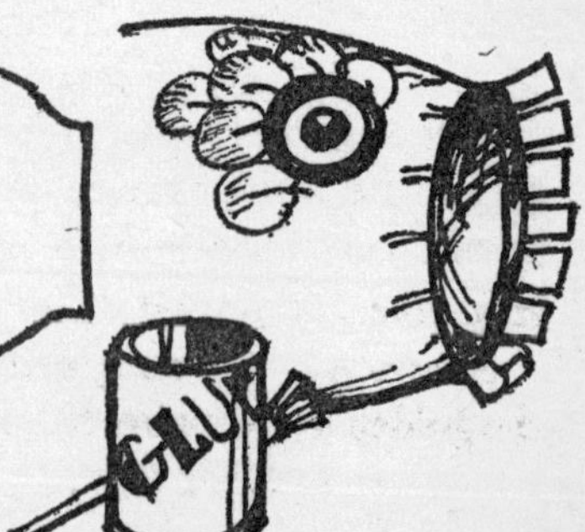

Fasten a long loop of thread from one side of the wire to the other, twisting the centre of the loop around the end of your bamboo stick, and fastening it firmly into place.

Now your fish is ready to fly. He will look very spectacular when his body fills out with wind, but treat him gently or he will get torn.

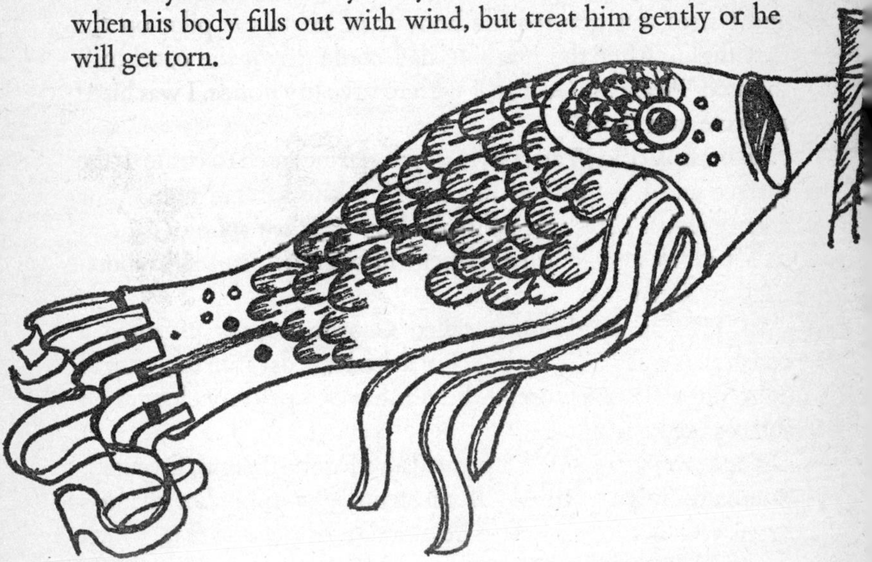

Kites

Kites were invented in China, possibly as long ago as one thousand years before Christ. In an ancient Chinese book, there is a description of 'a wooden bird' that stayed in the air for three days.

Men have always been fascinated by the idea of flying. The Chinese used kites for lifting bricks and tiles when working on houses, and it was quickly realised that if you built a big enough kite, it would be possible for men to fly by hanging from it. One Chinese Emperor used to punish prisoners by forcing them to fly, by kite, from the towers of his castle. If they managed to stay alive, he allowed them to go free.

A Japanese thief once used a kite to try to steal the scales from the golden dolphins on the roof of Nagoya Castle. The theft was successful, but he was later caught, and he and his family were boiled in oil.

In England, George Cayley built a glider lifted by kites over one hundred years ago. The man who normally drove his coach and horses was granted the honour of being the pilot on the first flight. After the machine had come down the coachman shouted 'Please Sir George, I wish to give my notice. I was hired to drive, not to fly'.

In both World Wars, German submarines used to come to the surface and hoist one of the crew by kite to scan the sea for enemy ships. Kites were also used by German spies in Britain to lift radio signalling equipment into the air, to send reports back to Germany.

In 1826 an Englishman called George Pocock invented a coach that was *pulled* by kite. It reached speeds of up to 35 km/h (20 mph). What is more, it did not have to pay any charges on toll roads and bridges.

Kites are still being improved, and new designs invented. Some are flown with weather instruments, to predict changes in the weather. In aircraft, a new design of ejection seat, which uses a kite instead of a parachute, helps a pilot to come down more safely. This is one type of man-lifting. Another type is used in the new and dangerous sport of hang-gliding, in which the pilot drives the kite hanging below it, in mid-air. And more people than ever are flying kites for fun.

Rainy-Day-Riddles

Q. What did the ground say to the rain?
A. If you carry on this way my name will be mud.

Q. Which is the worst weather for rats and mice?
A. When it's raining cats and dogs.

Q. How do you know when it's raining cats and dogs?
A. The ground is covered with poodles.

*Springburst**

(*Please read this from the bottom)

FLOWER!
the
slowly slowly
the *petal* curling
the *bud*,
awakening.

Oh, the
up!
straight
I know!
Now
hm.
see. hm see.
me Hm me
Let Let
higher . . .
must reach

for the sky –
Now, must reach
I be!
I live!

up
tip
warmth
coolness
water,
food and
life growing,
life, being,
in the dark –

(seed style)
spark
A

John Travers Moore

Cuckoo Song

Summer is y-comen in,
Loude sing, cuckoo!
Groweth seed and bloweth meed
And springeth the woode now –
Sing cuckoo!

Ewe bleateth after lamb,
Loweth after calfe cow;
Bullock starteth, bucke farteth,
Merry sing, cuckoo!

Cuckoo, Cuckoo!
Well singest thou, cuckoo:
Ne swike thou never now!
Sing cuckoo, now! Sing cuckoo!
Sing cuckoo! Sing, cuckoo, now!

Tongue-Twister

Some shun sunshine.

Barometer Bill

You will need:
one large, clean, pine cone
two pipe cleaners
plasticine
paper
a piece of cotton
strands of wool
glue
scissors

This is what you do:
Turn the cone upside down, and twist one pipe-cleaner around the thicker end, towards the top, to look like arms. Twist the other one around the bottom of the cone and bend the two ends down to look like legs, adding little plasticine feet.

Make a head by cutting a circle of tissue paper and shaping it into a ball stuffed with cotton wool or tissue and tied tightly with cotton.

Draw a smiling face on the head, and glue strands of wool into place to give Bill a mop of hair.

Now glue the head firmly on to the top of the body and give it a neat, finished look by cutting a stiff paper collar and fastening it into place to cover the join.

You will find that when the weather is dry Bill's pine cone body will open up. When it is wet he will look thin and smooth.

Summer day

We sat by the roadside and scooped the dust with our hands and made little piles in the gutters. Then we slid through the grass and lay on our backs and just stared at the empty sky. There was nothing to do. Nothing moved or happened, nothing happened at all except summer. Small heated winds blew over our faces, dandelion seeds floated by, burnt sap and roast nettles tinged our nostrils together with the dull rust smell of dry ground. The grass was June high, and had come up with a rush, a massed entanglement of species, crested with flowers and spears of wild wheat, and coiled with clambering vetches, the whole of it humming with blundering bees and flickering with scarlet butterflies. Chewing grass on our backs, the grass scaffolding the sky, the summer was all we heard; cuckoos crossed distances on chains of cries, flies buzzed and choked in the ears, and the saw-toothed chatter of mowing machines drifted on waves of air from the fields.

We moved. We went to the shop and bought sherbet and sucked it through sticks of liquorice. Sucked gently, the sherbet merely dusted the tongue; too hard, and you choked with sweet powders; if you blew back through the tube the sherbet-bag burst and you disappeared in a blizzard of sugar. Sucking and blowing, coughing and weeping, we scuffled our way down the lane. We drank at the spring to clean our mouths, then threw water at each other and made rainbows. Mr Jones's pond was bubbling with life, and covered with great white lilies – they poured from their leaves like candle-fat, ran molten, then cooled on the water. Moorhens plopped, and dabchicks scooted, insects rowed and skated. New-hatched frogs hopped about like flies, lizards gulped in the grass. The lane itself was crusted with cow-dung, hard-baked and smelling good.

from Cider With Rosie *by Laurie Lee*

Weathers

This is the weather the cuckoo likes,
And so do I;
When showers betumble the chestnut spikes,
And nestlings fly:
And the little brown nightingale bills his best,
And they sit outside at 'The Travellers' Rest',
And maids come forth sprig-muslin drest,
And citizens dream of the south and west,
And so do I.

This is the weather the shepherd shuns,
And so do I;
When beeches drip in browns and duns,
And thresh and ply:
And hill-hid tides throb, throe on throe,
And meadow rivulets overflow,
And drops on gate-bars hang in a row,
And rooks in families homeward go,
And so do I.

Thomas Hardy

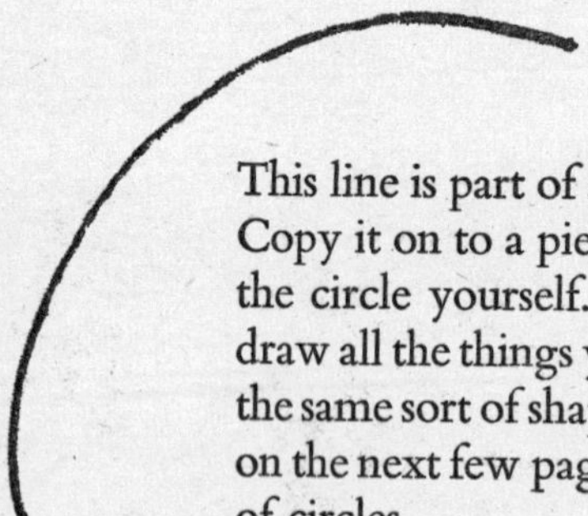

This line is part of a circle.
Copy it on to a piece of paper, and finish off the circle yourself. Underneath your circle draw all the things you can think of that have the same sort of shape. You'll find some clues on the next few pages to start your collection of circles.

Weather-Words . . .

Hark! I hear the asses bray;
We shall have some rain today.

If the cock crows on going to bed
He's sure to rise with a watery head.

If the moon shows a silver shield
Be not afraid to reap your field,
But if she rises haloed round
Soon we'll tread on deluged ground.

If it rains when the sun is shining, the devil is beating his wife.

A rainbow in the morning is the shepherd's warning.
A rainbow at night is the shepherd's delight.

When the rain raineth and the goose winketh
Little wots the gosling what the goose thinketh.

. . . and Warnings

If the sun in red should set
The next surely will be wet.
If the sun should set in grey
The next will be a rainy day.

Evening red and morning grey
Help the traveller on his way;
Evening grey and morning red
Bring down the rain upon his head.

If the oak's before the ash,
Then you'll only get a splash;
If the ash precedes the oak,
Then you may expect a soak.

Although it rain, throw not away thy watering pot.

If cold wind reach you through a hole
Say your prayers and mend your soul.

Ball Bouncing

Bounce ball! Bounce ball!
One, two, three.
Underneath my right leg
And round about my knee.
Bounce ball! Bounce ball!
Bird-or-bee
Flying from the rose-bud
Up into the tree.

Bounce ball! Bounce ball!
Fast-you-go.
Underneath my left leg
And round about my toe.
Bounce ball! Bounce ball!
Butt-er-fly
Flying from the rose-bud
Up into the sky.

Make a balloon head

You will need:
a jar
scissors
a balloon
petroleum jelly (vaseline)
tissue paper
newspaper
an egg carton
string or wool
wallpaper paste
glue and paints

This is what you do:

1. Blow up the balloon, tie a knot in the end, and stand it in the jar.
2. Spread it all over with a layer of petroleum jelly, then cover all this with torn-up pieces of tissue paper until you can't see any of the balloon.
3. Tear up newspapers into strips measuring about 20 cm by 2 cm, spread them with wallpaper paste, and glue them on to the balloon, making their edges overlap each other, and smoothing them down as you work. Go on doing this until there are about six layers of newspaper covering the balloon. Don't stop before you are finished, or it might collapse and then you'll have to start all over again.
4. Cut a nose out of an egg carton, glue it firmly into place, then put your balloon head into a warm place for about *one week* so that it can dry out completely and go quite hard.
5. After a week, burst the balloon and take it out of the inside of the head.
6. Now all you have to do is cut holes for eyes and mouth, paint on a face, and glue string or wool into place as hair.

If you prefer, you can cut the back off your balloon head and make it into a mask.

The Sun and the Wind

Once upon a time the sun and the wind had a quarrel because each one thought he was the most powerful.

'Look at me,' said the sun, 'I'm the greatest. I glow. I shine. I dazzle. All the people can see me riding in my glory high in the sky. As for you, Wind, you're nothing. Nothing but a puff of air.'

The wind was furious. 'Can a puff of air blow down trees, and whip the roofs off houses, and send chimney pots crashing down to the ground? A puff of air, indeed! Good gracious, I can toss big ships about on the ocean as if they were bathtime toys. I can make waves as big as mountains. *I* am the greatest.'

The sun got redder and redder he was so angry. 'I challenge you to a duel,' he blazed. 'There is a man down there, walking along the road. He's wearing a big, heavy coat, tightly buttoned up to his chin, and a long scarf wound round and around his neck. Whichever one of us manages to remove his coat and scarf is the winner.'

'Poof!' breezed the wind. 'That's easy. Just watch.' So he blew, and he blew, and he blew. He raged and he roared. He whistled, he whooped and he wailed. The trees bent double in the gale, the grass flattened itself to the ground, the little birds clustered together for comfort.

But the man turned up his collar, clutched his coat about him, and tucked his scarf firmly into his belt.

The sun laughed. 'My turn, my turn' he said. And he sailed out from behind a scudding cloud, and he shone, and he shone, and he shone. He gleamed down upon the earth with all his light and warmth. The leaves on the trees rustled with relief, the grass rippled happily, and the little birds twittered in the sunshine.

'Phew! that's better,' said the man, as he took off his scarf. 'My word, yes – that's much better,' he said, as he unbuttoned his coat. 'In fact,' he said, 'it's turned out a lovely day.' And he took off his coat, spread it on the grass, and lay down to sunbathe. 'There's nothing I like so much as a nice spot of sunshine,' he yawned. And then he fell asleep.

The sun beamed upon the wind, who had turned into a gentle little breeze. '*Now* who's the greatest?' he smiled.

Finger-Play

Five little peas in a pea-pod pressed, (*Clench fingers on one hand.*)
One grew, two grew, and so did all the rest. (*Raise fingers slowly.*)
They grew and grew and did not stop. (*Stretch fingers wide.*)
Until one day the pod went POP. (*Clap loudly on POP.*)

Make an owl-picture

You will need:
glue
rice
18 short pieces of spaghetti
white card
coloured paper
scissors

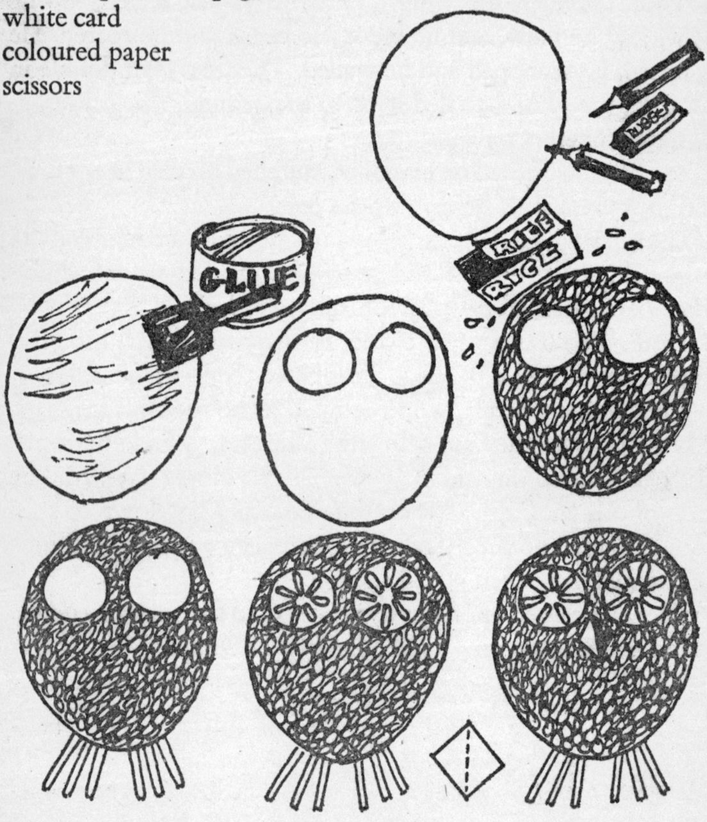

This is what you do:
1. Draw an egg-shape on your paper, the wide end at the top, and spread this shape with a thin layer of glue.
2. Cut two circles from your white card and lay them side by

side towards the top of your egg-shape. These will be the owl's eyes.
3. Cover the rest of the glue with a sprinkling of rice. These are his feathers.
4. At either side of the bottom of the shape glue three short pieces of spaghetti to look like claws.
5. On each of the circles glue six pieces of spaghetti, spreading out from the centre like spokes of a wheel.
6. Cut a small square of card, fold it from one corner to the opposite corner, then place it between the eyes, the fold running from top to bottom, to look like a beak.

Grow peas in a jar

You will need:
a jar
3 dried peas
blotting paper
scissors
water
sawdust or cottonwool
a cup

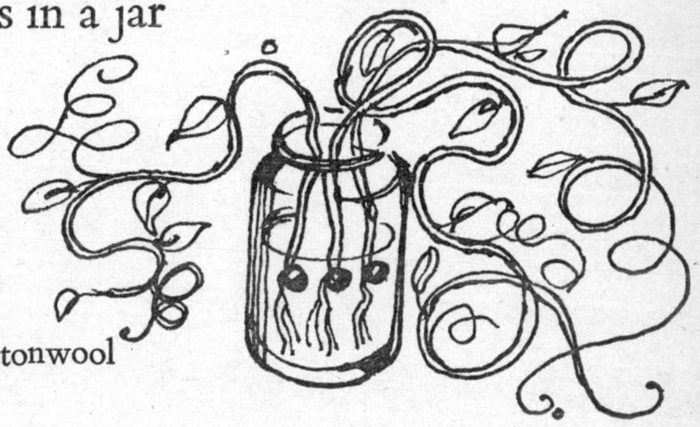

This is what you do:
1. Put the dried peas in a cup of cold water and leave for a day.
2. Cut the blotting paper into an oblong to fit into the inside of the jar, and put it into position.
3. Fill the jar three-quarters full with sawdust or cottonwool, and wet it.
4. Push your peas down the side of the jar, between the glass and the blotting paper.
5. Put your jar in a light place and keep the sawdust or cottonwool damp. Soon roots will start to grow, and then leaves and tendrils.

Woolloomooloo

Here's a ridiculous riddle for you:
How many o's are in Woolloomooloo?
Two for the W, two for the m,
Four for the l's, and that's plenty for them.

C. J. Dennis

Johnny went to church one day,
He climbed up in the steeple;
He took his shoes and stockings off
And threw them at the people.

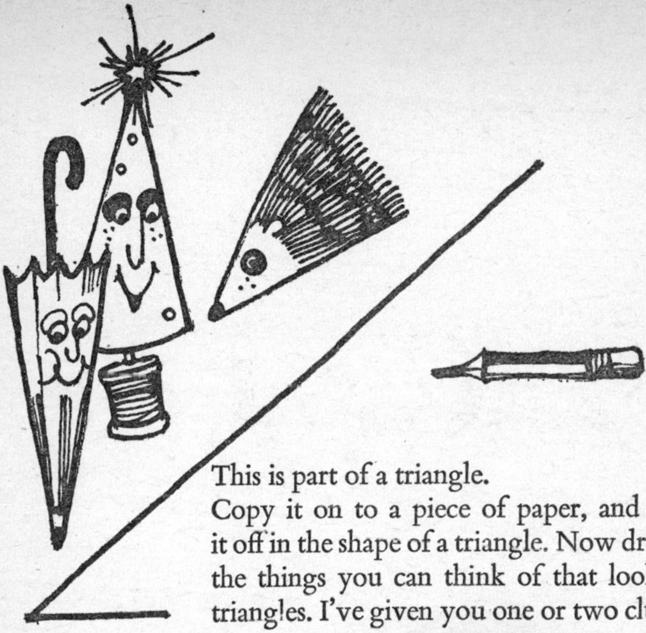

This is part of a triangle.
Copy it on to a piece of paper, and finish it off in the shape of a triangle. Now draw all the things you can think of that look like triangles. I've given you one or two clues.

Finger Play

Here's the church	*(Interlace your fingers, finger-tips downwards, and palms touching.)*
And here's the steeple	*(Point your first fingers together, and make them touch.)*
Open the door and out come the people.	*(Turn your hands upwards and wriggle your fingers.)*
Here's the church cat	*(Clench your right hand, and raise your thumb and little finger for ears.)*
And her kittens four,	*(Hold up four fingers of your left hand.)*
Watch them as they scamper Right across the floor.	*(Run your fingers across the table.)*

Make a witch's hat

You will need:
6 sheets of newspaper
wallpaper paste
scissors
pencil
black paint

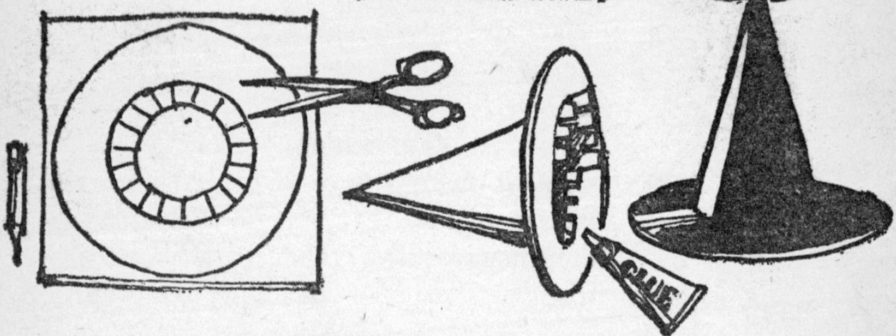

This is what you do:

1. Paste three sheets of newspaper together, on top of each other, then paste the other three together in the same way, and leave them to one side until they are quite dry.
2. From one piece cut as large a half-circle as you possibly can.
3. Twist this into a cone large enough to fit on to your head, and glue the sides together.
4. Stand this cone on your second piece of paper and draw around the bottom edge so that you have a big circle.
5. Now draw a second circle about 25 cm wider than the first one, and a third circle 5 cm smaller than the first one.
6. Cut around circles two and three, then make little snips all around the inside edge.
7. Spread some glue around the bottom edge of the cone, then slip the brim over the top and slide it down into place. You will find that the snips open out a little, and you must press them firmly against the side of the hat.
8. When the glue dries, paint the hat black.

Two Witches

There was a witch
The witch had an itch
The itch was so itchy it
Gave her a twitch.

Another witch
Admired the twitch
So she started twitching
Though she had no itch.

Now both of them twitch
So it's hard to tell which
Witch has the itch and
Which witch has the twitch.

Alexander Resnikoff

Teasers

Two sets of triangles to tease your brains.
How many triangles are there in this diagram? Don't give up too soon – there are probably more than you imagine.

(see page 144
for the answer)

You'll need seven matches for this one.
Here you see seven matches making four triangles.

Now try to rearrange them in a different way so that they still make up four triangles. It's easy – once you know how.

(see page 144 for the answer)

This is part of a square. Copy it, and complete it on a piece of paper, and then draw all the things you can think of that are square-shaped. Some hints are given above.

Alice meets the Red Queen

Alice had not been walking a minute before she found herself face to face with the Red Queen, and full in sight of the hill she had been so long aiming at.

'Where do you come from?' said the Red Queen. 'And where are you going? Look up, speak nicely, and don't twiddle your fingers all the time.'

Alice attended to all these directions, and explained, as well as she could, that she had lost her way.

'I don't know what you mean by *your* way,' said the Queen: 'all the ways about here belong to *me* – but why did you come out here at all?' she added in a kinder tone. 'Curtsey while you're thinking what to say. It saves time.'

Alice wondered a little at this, but she was too much in awe of the Queen to disbelieve it. 'I'll try it when I go home,' she thought to herself, 'the next time I'm a little late for dinner.'

'It's time for you to answer now,' the Queen said, looking at her watch: 'open your mouth a *little* wider when you speak, and always say "your Majesty".'

'I only wanted to see what the garden was like, your Majesty –'

'That's right,' said the Queen, patting her on the head, which Alice didn't like at all: 'though, when you say "garden", *I*'ve seen gardens, compared with which this would be a wilderness.'

Alice didn't dare to argue the point, but went on: '– and I thought I'd try and find my way to the top of that hill –'

'When you say "hill",' the Queen interrupted, 'I could show you hills, in comparison with which you'd call that a valley.'

'No, I shouldn't,' said Alice, surprised into contradicting her at last: 'a hill *can't* be a valley, you know. That would be nonsense –'

The Red Queen shook her head. 'You may call it "nonsense" if you like,' she said, 'but *I've* heard nonsense, compared with which that would be as sensible as a dictionary!'

Alice curtseyed again, as she was afraid from the Queen's tone that she was a *little* offended: and they walked on in silence till they got to the top of the little hill.

For some minutes Alice stood without speaking, looking out in all directions over the country – and a most curious country it was. There were a number of little brooks running across from side to side, and the ground between was divided up into squares by a number of hedges, that reached from brook to brook.

'I declare it's marked out just like a large chess-board!' Alice said at last. 'There ought to be some men moving about somewhere – and so there are!' she added in a tone of delight, and her heart began to beat quick with excitement as she went on. 'It's a great game of chess that's being played – all over the world – if this *is* the world at all, you know. Oh, what fun it is! How I *wish* I was one of them! I wouldn't mind being a Pawn, if only I might join – though of course I should *like* to be a Queen, best.'

from Alice Through the Looking Glass *by Lewis Carroll*

Two Magic Squares

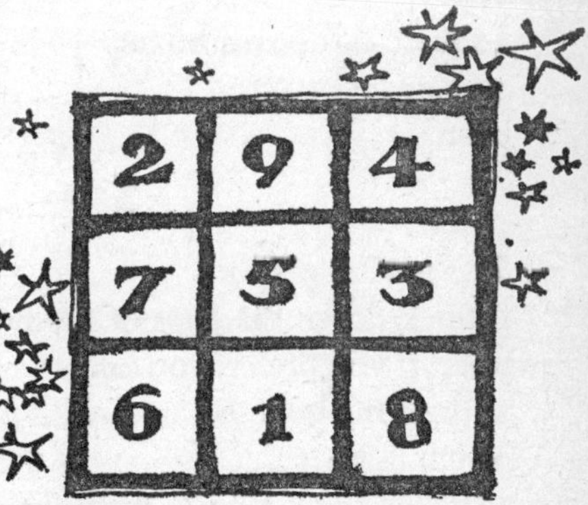

This is a very clever number square.
If you do a few simple sums you'll see that the numbers in any row, up and down, side to side, or corner to corner always add up to the same figure. What is it?

(see page 144 for the answer)

This one is even cleverer.

All the four lines across, all the four lines up and down, and the two from corner to corner add up to the same total – 34. But there's more to it than that. Each group of four small squares – there are nine altogether – also adds up to 34. Try it and see.

Make yourself some giant dice

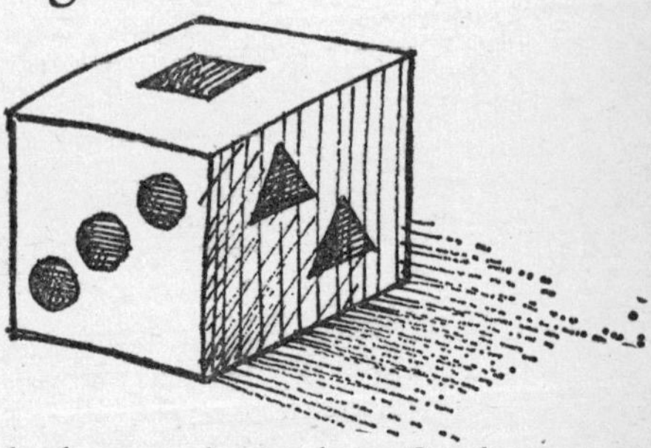

You will need:
2 square cardboard boxes
glue or sticky tape
paints

This is what you do:

1. Stick down the flaps of the boxes, gluing them firmly into place. If you prefer, you can fasten them down with sticky tape.
2. Paint the boxes all over with brightly coloured poster paint, or emulsion paint.
3. When they are dry, paint the sides with squares, circles and triangles instead of dots.

Remember that the 6 must be opposite the 1, the 5 opposite the 2, and the 4 opposite the 3.

4. Finish off by painting a border round all the edges of the dice in a contrasting colour.

Make yourself some useful boxes

You will need:
cardboard boxes, any shape and size, but preferably square-ish
pictures cut from magazines, birthday cards, etc
scissors
glue
sticky tape
paint

This is what you do

1. Make each box strong and firm by taping all the joins except for the opening flap which you will probably want to keep as a lid.
2. Cover all the outside of the box, and the inside of the lid, with a coat of paint.
3. When they are quite dry, cover all the painted surfaces with cut-outs.

Pile up the boxes on top of each other and they will not only be useful for storing your things, they will also look smart.

The Three Foxes

Once upon a time there were three little foxes
Who didn't wear stockings, and they didn't wear sockses,
But they all had handkerchiefs in cardboard boxes.

They lived in the forest in three little houses,
And they didn't wear coats, and they didn't wear trousies.
They ran through the woods on their little bare tootsies,
And they played 'touch last' with a family of mouses.

They didn't go shopping in the High Street shopses,
But caught what they wanted in the woods and copses.
They all went fishing, and they caught three wormses,
They went out hunting, and they caught three wopses.

They went to a Fair, and they all won prizes –
Three plum-puddingses and three mince-pieses.
They rode on elephants and swang on swingses,
And hit three coco-nuts at coco-nut shieses.

That's all that I know of the three little foxes
Who kept their handkerchiefs in cardboard boxes.
They lived in the forest in three little houses,
But they didn't wear coats and they didn't wear trousies.
And they didn't wear stockings and they didn't wear sockses.

A. A. Milne

Make yourself a box-mobile

You will need:
tiny decorated boxes,
with their lids fastened down
a pretty coat hanger
thread
little bells

This is what you do:
Put threads through the tops of two or three little boxes, so that you can hang them from the hanger. Fasten a little bell to the bottom of each box. Now fasten up the mobile near a door or window and whenever there is a breeze it will twirl and tinkle. This would make a splendid present, especially for a baby.

Teaser

More matches.

Here are twelve matches arranged to make four squares. Now take four of the matches away and put them into different positions so that your twelve matches make three squares.

(for the answer see page 144)

Picture Shapes

The warm yellow sun,
The moon when it's full,
A bright red balloon,
A big bouncing ball
– And bubbles.
Circles.

A kite in the sky,
A witch's tall hat,
The signs by the road,
My crisp ice-cream cone
– And spires.
Triangles.

A box for my things
Like handkies and stamps,
My chess board and dice,
Blocks, crosswords and draughts
– And sugar-lumps.
Squares.

J. Greenawe

Children waking

'I see a ring,' said Bernard, 'hanging above me. It quivers and hangs in a loop of light.'

'I see a slab of pale yellow,' said Susan, 'spreading away until it meets a purple stripe.'

'I hear a sound,' said Rhoda, 'cheep, chirp; cheep, chirp; going up and down.'

'I see a globe,' said Neville, 'hanging down in a drop against the enormous flanks of some hill.'

'I see a crimson tassel,' said Jinny, 'twisted with gold threads.'

'I hear something stamping,' said Louis. 'A great beast's foot is chained. It stamps, and stamps, and stamps.'

'Look at the spider's web on the corner of the balcony,' said

Bernard. 'It has beads of water on it, drops of white light.'

'The leaves are gathered round the window like pointed ears,' said Susan.

'A shadow falls on the path,' said Louis, 'like an elbow bent.'

'Islands of light are swimming on the grass,' said Rhoda. 'They have fallen through the trees.'

'The birds' eyes are bright in the tunnels between the leaves,' said Neville.

'The stalks are covered with harsh, short hairs,' said Jinny, 'and drops of water have stuck to them.'

'A caterpillar is curled in a green ring,' said Susan, 'notched with blunt feet.'

'The grey-shelled snail draws across the path and flattens the blades behind him,' said Rhoda.

'And burning lights from the window-panes flash in and out on the grasses,' said Louis.

'Stones are cold to my feet,' said Neville. 'I feel each one, round or pointed, separately.'

'The back of my hand burns,' said Jinny, 'but the palm is clammy and damp with dew.'

'Now the cock crows like a spurt of hard, red water in the white tide,' said Bernard.

'Birds are singing up and down and in and out all round us,' said Susan.

'The beast stamps; the elephant with its foot chained; the great brute on the beach stamps,' said Louis.

'Look at the house,' said Jinny, 'with all its windows white with blinds.'

'Cold water begins to run from the scullery tap,' said Rhoda, 'over the mackerel in the bowl.'

'The walls are cracked with gold cracks,' said Bernard, 'and there are blue, finger-shaped shadows of leaves beneath the windows.'

'Now Mrs Constable pulls up her thick black stockings,' said Susan.

'When the smoke rises, sleep curls off the roof like a mist,' said Louis.

'The birds sang in chorus first,' said Rhoda. 'Now the scullery door is unbarred. Off they fly. Off they fly like a fling of seed. But one sings by the bedroom window alone.'

'Bubbles form on the floor of the saucepan,' said Jinny. 'Then they rise, quicker and quicker, in a silver chain to the top.'

'Now Biddy scrapes the fish-scales with a jagged knife on to a wooden board,' said Neville.

'The dining-room window is dark blue now,' said Bernard, 'and the air ripples above the chimneys.'

'A swallow is perched on the lightning-conductor,' said Susan. 'And Biddy has smacked down the bucket on the kitchen flags.'

'That is the first stroke of the church bell,' said Louis. 'Then the others follow; one, two; one, two; one, two.'

'Look at the table-cloth, flying along the table,' said Rhoda. 'Now there are rounds of white china, and silver streaks beside each plate.'

'Suddenly a bee booms in my ear,' said Neville. 'It is here; it is past.'

'I burn, I shiver,' said Jinny, 'out of this sun, into this shadow.'

'Now they have all gone,' said Louis. 'I am alone. They have gone into the house for breakfast, and I am left standing by the wall among the flowers. It is very early, before lessons. Flower after flower is specked on the depths of green. The petals are harlequins. Stalks rise from the black hollows beneath. The flowers swim like fish made of light upon the dark, green waters.'

from The Waves *by Virginia Woolf*

The Dripping Tap

Drip drap
Goes the dripping tap,
Drip drap!

Flit flot
Into the old jampot,
Flit flot!

Plashes plishes
Over the unwashed dishes,
Plashes plishes!

Dillery dullery
All over the scullery,
Dillery dullery!

Tink tonk tank
On the draining-board plank,
Tink tonk tank!

Bink bankety bunk
On a pile of junk,
Bink bankety bunk!

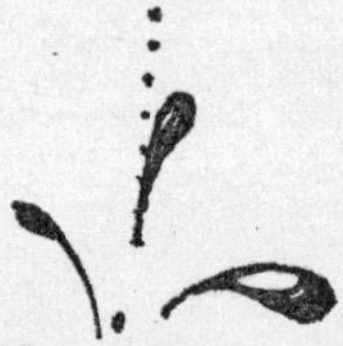

Junk in the sink?
That's a bit odd, I think,
Junk in the sink!

But so is the pink
Of a dripping tap in the kitchen sink,
Pink! Pink! Pink!

James Kirkup

Playground Rhymes for Starting a Game

One-ery, oo-ry, ick-ry, an,
Bipsy, bopsy, little Sir Jan,
Queery, quaury,
Virgin Mary,
Nick, tick, toloman tick,
O-U-T, out,
Rotten, totten, dish-clout,
Out jumps – *He*.

Ickledee, pickledee, elleka-mah,
Dex Q elleka-fah,
Awnty Sawnty, elleka-see,
Trance.

The Bewildered Breakfast

Waiter: And what would you like for breakfast, sir?
Gentleman: I'll have a cup of tea and a muttered buffin.
Waiter: You mean a buffered mutton?
Gentleman: No, you fool. I mean tea and a muffered button!
Waiter: Oh dear. What about coast and toffee instead?

Two Tooters

A tutor who tooted the flute
Tried to tutor two tooters to toot.
  Said the two to the tutor,
  'Is it harder to toot, or
To tutor two tooters to toot?'

Farmyard treasure

A noisy, funny party game for a small group of children. You can play it either in the house or in the garden.

First of all, you need to choose a farmer. The farmer then gives each player the name of a farmyard animal. If there are five of you, for instance, he might choose a donkey, a sheep, a duck, a cow and a dog. He then describes to each player the sort of 'treasure' he must look for. Perhaps the donkey will be searching for pebbles, the cow's treasure might be marbles, the others could be looking for sweets, sugar lumps or beans. Each one has to find five pieces of his own particular treasure, which will have been hidden, before the game begins, around the house or garden.

As soon as the farmer shouts 'Seek, seek' all the players hurry off to look for their treasure. However, when they do find a piece they must not touch it. Instead, they stand beside it and make the sound of the animal they represent until the farmer comes along to collect it and put it in his basket.

The winner is the player who first manages to get his five pieces of treasure into the farmer's basket.

Two Tongue-Twister Games

1. For two players.

The first player thinks of a tongue-twister, and says it to his partner. The partner then has to repeat it five times, quickly. If either one of them stumbles over the words, he loses the game. If neither player, or both, twist their tongues, it is a draw. Then it is the second player's turn to think of a tongue-twister for his partner to repeat five times.

See who can win most games.

2. For a group of players.

The first player invents a tongue-twister of three words, and says it to the next player, who has to repeat it three times, quickly, and then pass it on to the third player, with one word added at the beginning or the end. Carry on in this way until everyone in the group has had a turn. Players are out of the game if they make a mistake, or are too slow. The game finishes when there is only one player left.

Make a windmobile

You will need:
16 foil lids from yogurt
or cream cartons
strong thread
scissors
glue
a short bamboo cane, or straight stick

This is what you do:

Lay out your foil circles in a square made up of four lines of four.

Cut four long lengths of thread and glue each piece to one of the rows of tops, leaving a space of about 3 cm between the edges.

Tie each of the four threads to the cane, making sure that the circles are spaced in such a way that they just touch those fastened on to the next thread.

Fasten a piece of string from one end of the cane to the other in a loop, and slip this on to the branch of a tree.

When the wind blows your windmobile should sparkle and make a gentle chiming sound as it moves.

A Trio of Tricky Tongue-Twisters

Five frolicsome fairies fanned a fainting flea.

Some shy and slippery seals slithered ashore, shivering.

Bandy-legged Borachio Mustachio Whiskerifusticus, the Bald and Brave Bombandino of Baghdad, helped Abomilque Bluebeard Bashaw of Babelmandel to beat down an abominable bumblebee at Balsora.

Ned Nott and Sam Shott

Ned Nott was shot
  and Sam Shott was not.
So it is better to be Shott
  than Nott.
Some say Nott
  was *not* shot.
But Shott says
  he shot Nott.
Either the shot Shott shot at Nott
  was not shot
  or
  Nott was shot.
If the shot Shott shot shot Nott,
  Nott was shot.
But if the shot Shott shot shot Shott,
  then Shott was shot,
  not Nott.
However,
  the shot Shott shot shot not Shott –
  but Nott.

Spring

Spring, the sweet Spring, is the year's pleasant king;
Then blooms each thing, then maids dance in a ring,
Cold doth not sting, the pretty birds do sing,
Cuckoo, jug, jug, pu we, to witta woo.

The palm and may make country houses gay,
Lambs frisk and play, the shepherds pipe all day,
And we hear aye birds tune this merry lay,
Cuckoo, jug, jug, pu we, to witta woo.

The fields breathe sweet, the daisies kiss our feet,
Young lovers meet, old wives a-sunning sit,
In every street these tunes our ears do greet,
Cuckoo, jug, jug, pu we, to witta woo.

Thomas Nashe

Wit. Wit. Willy. Willy.

Till I lived in the Daye House I had no idea of how elaborate is the language used by birds. Thrushes especially have an immense vocabulary; and I copied down one morning, as carefully as I could, the actual words sung by a thrush in the laburnum outside my window. This was his song:

Wit. Wit. Willy, Willy, Wit
Tchelitchef. Tchelitchef.
O-o-o-oy.
Dirt. Dirt. Dirt.
Birdy, birdy, pretty birdy
Quick. Quick.
Give me a liqueur. Give me a liqueur.
Tch. Tch. Tch.
He's wheeling in tea and balloons.
See. See. See.
Be brave. Be brave.
Wor-r-rds. Wor-r-rds. Wor-r-rds.
Be a cheat. Be a cheat.
Give me some tea.
Just now. Just now.
I've been wet. I've been wet.
Not a word. Not a wor-r-rd.
Beer. Beer. Beer.
No he won't. No he won't.
Happy. Happy.
Wobble a woodle too.
Piano. Piano.
Cruel. Cruel.
Stand. Come here.
Did you see? Did you see?
Boys boiling in oil.
Willy cot. Willy say
Oh we know. Oh we know.
We go wheeling along.

Se-e-e. Where is he? See sir. See sir.
Let me kiss you.
Chicken beef and ham
Give him gurls. Give him gurls.
Is he going to scream! to scream?
What a spree! What a spree!

Edith Olivier

Make your own music

Here are four simple musical instruments for you to make and play.

1 A slither box

You will need:
a small box or tin
adhesive tape
two or three handfuls of
dried peas or pasta shapes

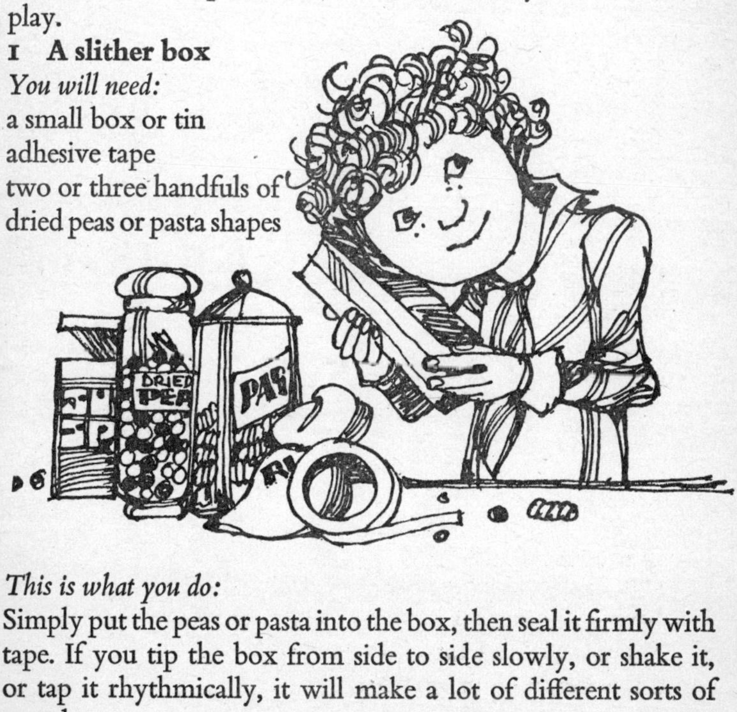

This is what you do:
Simply put the peas or pasta into the box, then seal it firmly with tape. If you tip the box from side to side slowly, or shake it, or tap it rhythmically, it will make a lot of different sorts of sounds.

2 A jingle stick

You will need:

about 30 metal bottle tops
a wooden pole or broomstick
a screwdriver
a hammer
glue
a piece of cork
30 nails

This is what you do:

Prise out the cork or plastic from the inside of each bottle top with the screwdriver then, using a hammer and nail, make a hole in the centre of each one, and nail them on to the top end of the pole making sure that they have room to move around freely.
Glue a piece of cork on to the bottom of the pole.
When you bang your jingle stick on the ground it will make a pleasant chiming sound.

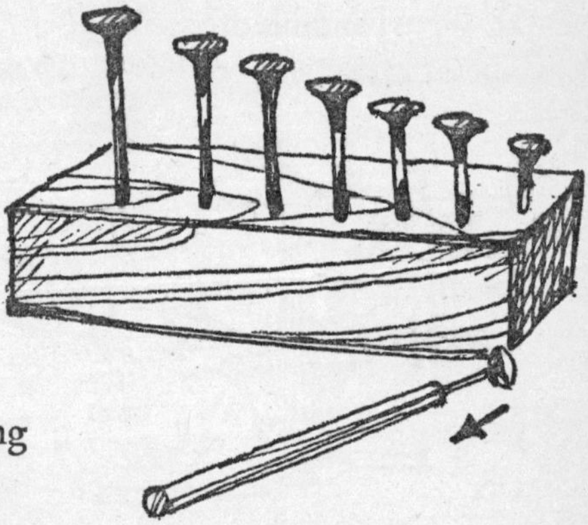

3 A xylophone

You will need:

a sold block of wood
9 long nails
a hammer
a short piece of dowelling

This is what you do:

Hammer eight nails into the block of wood in a row, starting with one that is hammered well down and ending with one that is about twice as tall, and you should be able to play a scale.
To make a hammer to play your xylophone, knock a nail into the end of the dowelling.

4 A sounding box

All you need is:
a wooden or cardboard box, without a lid
4 strong elastic bands

All you do is:
Stretch the elastic bands over the longest side of the box, and pluck them, as if you were playing a guitar, to make a twanging sound.

The Sea Ritual

Prayer unsaid, and Mass unsung,
Deadman's dirge must still be rung:
  Dingle-dong, the dead-bells sound!
  Mermen chant his dirge around!

Wash him bloodless, smooth him fair,
Stretch his limbs, and sleek his hair:
  Dingle-dong, the dead-bells go!
  Mermen swing them to and fro!

In the wormless sand shall he
Feast for no foul gluttons be:
  Dingle-dong, the dead-bells chime!
  Mermen keep the tone and time!

We must with a tombstone brave
Shut the shark out from his grave:
  Dingle-dong, the dead-bells toll!
  Mermen dirgers ring his knoll!

Such a slab will we lay o'er him
All the dead shall rise before him!
  Dingle-dong, the dead-bells boom!
  Mermen lay him in his tomb!

George Darley

Make your own telephone

You will need:
2 coffee or cocoa tins, without any sharp edges
a long piece of string
a hammer
a nail

This is what you do:
Pierce a small hole in the centre of the bottom of each tin by hammering the nail through it, but be careful not to make a dent. Now thread the string through the holes and tie a knot on the end inside the tin so that it cannot be pulled out.

If your friend holds one tin to his ear while you pull the string tight and then speak into the other tin he will be able to hear what you say quite clearly. You will not need to shout, but if you speak in a high voice it will carry along the string more easily.

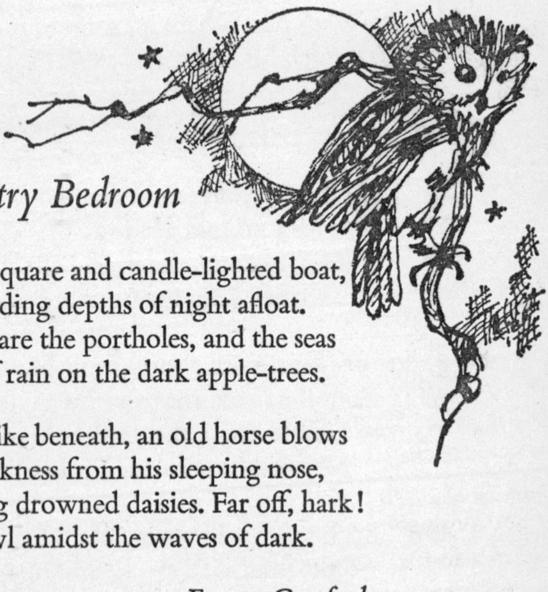

The Country Bedroom

My room's a square and candle-lighted boat,
In the surrounding depths of night afloat.
My windows are the portholes, and the seas
The sounds of rain on the dark apple-trees.

Sea monster-like beneath, an old horse blows
A snort of darkness from his sleeping nose,
Below, among drowned daisies. Far off, hark!
Far off one owl amidst the waves of dark.

Frances Cornford

A Spell for Sleeping

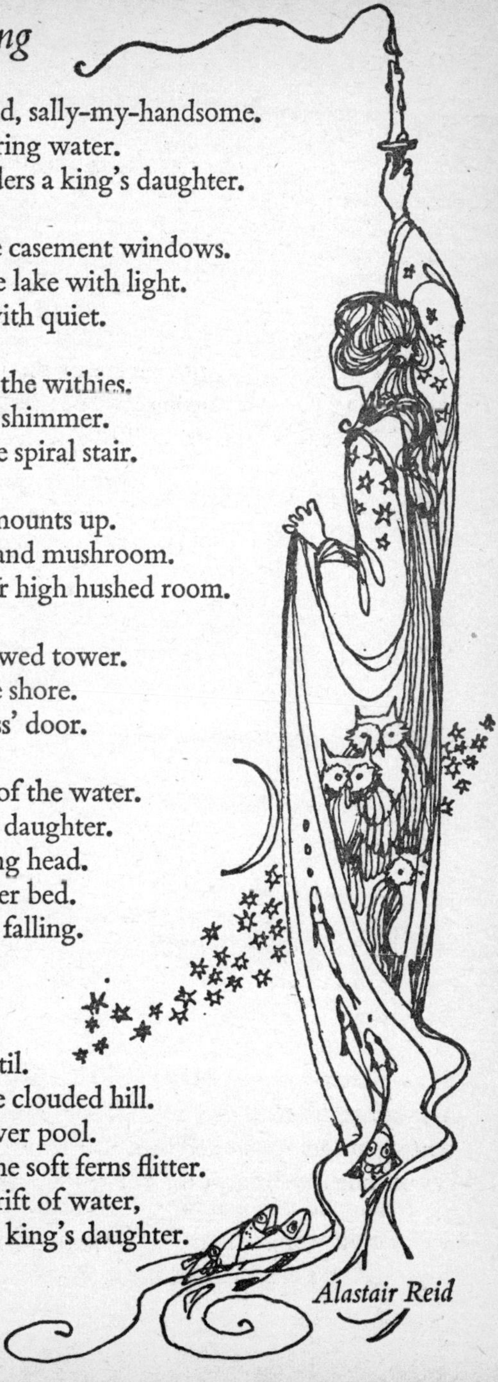

Sweet william, silverweed, sally-my-handsome.
Dimity darkens the pittering water.
On gloomed lawns wanders a king's daughter.

Curtains are clouding the casement windows.
A moon-glade smurrs the lake with light.
Doves cover the tower with quiet.

Three owls whit-whit in the withies.
Seven fish in a deep pool shimmer.
The princess moves to the spiral stair.

Slowly the sickle moon mounts up.
Frogs hump under moss and mushroom.
The princess climbs to her high hushed room.

Step by step to her shadowed tower.
Water laps the white lake shore.
A ghost opens the princess' door.

Seven fish in the sway of the water.
Six candles for a king's daughter.
Five sighs for a drooping head.
Four ghosts to gentle her bed.
Three owls in the dusk falling.
Two tales to be telling.
One spell for sleeping.

Tamarisk, trefoil, tormentil.
Sleep rolls down from the clouded hill.
A princess dreams of a silver pool.
The moonlight spreads, the soft ferns flitter.
Stilled in a shimmering drift of water,
Seven fish dream of a lost king's daughter.

Alastair Reid

Things

Trains are for going,
Boats are for rowing,
Seeds are for sowing,
Noses for blowing,
And sleeping's for bed.

Dogs are for pawing,
Logs are for sawing,
Crows are for cawing,
Rivers for thawing,
And sleeping's for bed.

Flags are for flying,
Stores are for buying,
Glasses for spying,
Babies for crying,
And sleeping's for bed.

Cows are for mooing,
Chickens for shooing,
Blue is for bluing,
Things are for doing,
And sleeping's for bed.

Games are for playing,
Hay is for haying,
Horses for neighing,
Sayings for saying,
And sleeping's for bed.

Money's for spending,
Patients for tending,
Branches for bending,
Poems for ending,
And sleeping's for bed.

William Jay Smith

Night Sounds

Midnight's bell goes ting, ting, ting,
Then dogs do howl, and not a bird does sing
But the nightingale, and she cries twit, twit, twit;
Owls then on every bough do sit;
Ravens croak on chimneys' tops;
The cricket in the chamber hops;
The nibbling mouse is not asleep,
But he goes peep, peep, peep, peep, peep;
  And the cats cry mew, mew, mew,
  And still the cats cry mew, mew, mew.

Thomas Middleton

End piece

Q. What did the beaver say to the tree?
A. It's been nice gnawing you.

Answers

Page 117
There are 35 triangles in the diagram.

Page 118

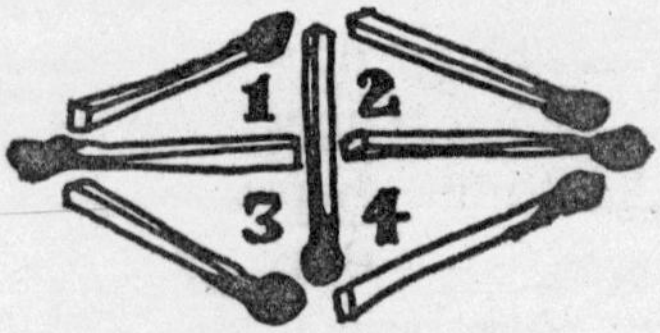

Page 121

1. All the numbers in any row add up to 15.

Page 125
The matches represented by dotted lines are removed and positioned to make one square.

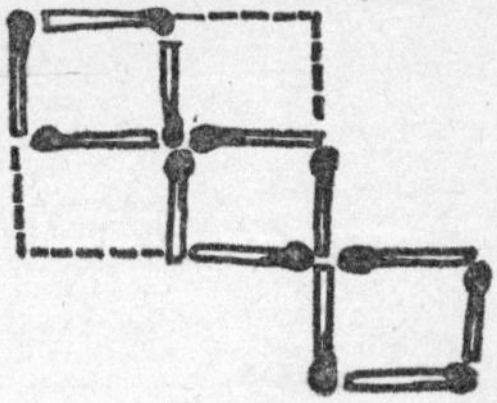

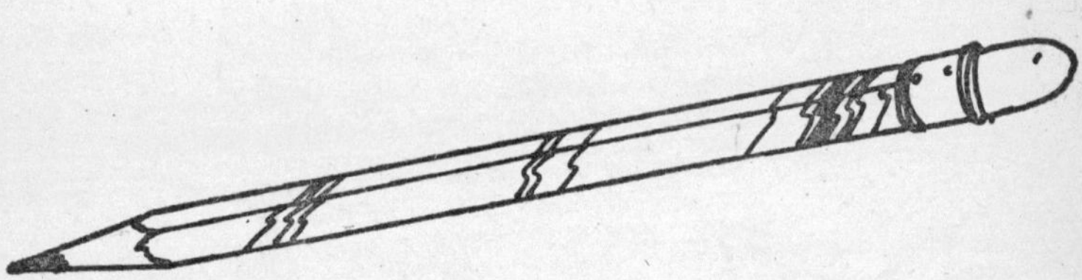

New Beavers are published every month and if you would like the *Beaver Bulletin* – which gives all the details – please send a large stamped addressed envelope to:

Beaver Bulletin
The Hamlyn Group
Astronaut House
Feltham
Middlesex TW14 9AR

371344